AN AGENDA OF ECONOMIC REFORMS FOR THE STATES IN INDIA

AN AGENDA OF ECONOMIC REFORMS FOR THE STATES IN INDIA

V. B. Jugale

SERIALS PUBLICATIONS
NEW DELHI

First Published - 2008

ISBN: 978-81-8387-185-3

Published by

SERIALS PUBLICATIONS
4830/24, Prahlad Street, Ansari Road
Darya Ganj, New Delhi-110002 (India)
Phone : 23245225. Fax : 91-11-23272135
E-mail: serials@satyam.net.in

CONTENTS

PREFACE

The economic reforms introduced since 1990's have been proved to be a boon for the uplifting of the Indian economy. The rising GDP growth rate, expanding forex, employment generation in IT and communication sectors has brought a new boulevard in the socio- economic life of the country. The macro economic reforms at the initial levels were criticized by various individuals and organizations, but now a favorable environment has been generated. The public support to the reforms is a reward to the government's policies. The macro level agenda of reforms have been now transformed to the State level agencies. The States are held responsible for implementing the missing agenda of socio-economic reforms. It is an opportunity as well as a challenge to the state governments. However, a visionary plan with perspective approach towards socio- economic transformation will definitely guide the state agencies. With a view to enlighten the state level agenda of economic reforms, the Department of Economics Shivaji University Kolhapur, has organized a national level seminar on an agenda of economic reforms for the states in India in March 2005. Diversified items of agendas have been presented by the national expertise. Eminent discussants were specially invited as discussants on the themes.

An agricultural development agenda for the Western Maharashtra has been presented by Professor V. B. Jugale. Precision agriculture has a great amount of scope and perspectives to the state of Maharashtra. An agenda for co-operation was offered by M. V. Madane. The co-operation in fact, never fails but the co-operators fail. The selfish aphorism of the co-operators has to be removed for the healthy development of the collective action sector in India. R. R. Doshi has discussed the issues as above and over ruled the need of the state support with the matching public and private investments in the core sector of the state economies. The agricultural distress can only be minimized through visionary initiatives of the state agencies. Irrigation reforms in Maharashtra have been presented by S. G. Bhogale. The State's structural approach towards viable agriculture through proper irrigation policies has been justified as a right step towards the state's development agenda. A. R. Padoshi highlighted the states' agenda for agricultural credit. The co-operative credit as the best credit needs to be restructured under the financial sector reforms initiated at the macro level in India. D. M. More; an irrigation expert and an administrator have rightly pointed out the urge of public-private participation in the distribution of water resources. The Water User's Associations have been proved to be the best strategy of water distribution in Maharashtra and Andhra Pradesh.

M. G. Basavraj and et al have enlightened the infrastructural urge in Karnataka state. R. Y. Mahore has presented a thought provoking paper on higher education under the TRIPs regime. He honestly identified the states' responsibilities for maintaining the quality and competency of higher education in the Indian states. P. R. Wadje has introduced the textile agenda for Maharashtra state. The State's efforts in the textile development have been accounted in the light of MFA and WTO. J. F. Patil has summarized the observations and placed a vital agenda of the industrial growth in the state of Maharashtra.

R. P. Kurulkar has sincerely narrated the story of regional disparities in the growth process and urged the need to reduce it through state's efforts on a priority basis. V. S. Kulkarni; a practical banker has identified the states' role and participation in financial sector reforms. Banking as an important organ of the body economy and a nerve for vehementing the banking services should create a confidence and courage among the customers through the state invitation. K. Ramesh has thoroughly discussed the issues related to the regional disparities and the banking sector reforms in India.

He confessed the role of the states in removing the structural and banking sector disparities in the state economies.

M. Narsimhulu has presented a master piece of the agenda on fiscal reforms. The states have extensive opportunities in restructuring the tax base and revision of the tax rates. VAT is an opportunity to the states for improving their economic conditions. A. A. Dange reiterated the case of state finances within the system of financial reforms and expressed the qualms of growing state debts. M. C. Kodli; as an expert discussant commented on the papers with guiding principles for the states' fiscal reforms. The states should move towards the change in their fiscal powers vis-a-vis their implementation.

The papers discussed in the volume have honestly expressed the sensible views with guiding principles for the development of the states in India. The readers will definitely enjoy it.

The editor is very grateful to S. K Jha and his Serials family for publishing the papers on the thrust issues of the states in India. The editor is also very thankful to the officials and Department colleagues of the Shivaji University for their physical and moral assistance and encouragement.

V. B. Jugale
Kolhapur Professor,
Diwali Padava Editor

LIST OF CONTRIBUTORS

Dr. V.B. Jugale; Professor and Head, Department of Economics, Shivaji University, Kolhapur.

Madhav V. Madane; President, Indian Society for Studies in Co-operatives C/o Vamnicom, Pune.

R.R. Doshi; Former Professor & Head Department of Economics, Shivaji University, Kolhapur.

Dr. S.G. Bhogle; Rtd. Professor & Head, Faculty of Social Sciences, Walmi, Aurangabad.

Dr. A.R. Padoshi; Ex. Head, Department of Economics, Goa University, Goa.

D.M. More; Director General, Maharashtra Engineering Research Institute & Engineering Staff College, Dindori Road, Nasik.

Dr. M.G. Basava Raja; Department of Economics, University of Mysore, Sir M. Visvesvaraya, P.G. Centre, Mandya.

T. Ramesh, Manu Mahesh & M.D. Umesh; Research Scholars, University of Mysore, Sir M. Visvesvaraya, P.G. Centre, Mandya.

Dr. R.Y. Mahore; Professor, Department of Economics Nagpur University, Nagpur.

P.R. Wadje; Sr. Lecture in Economics, D.K.T.E.S.'s Textile & Engineering Institute, 'Rajwada', ICHALKARANJI, Dist. Kolhapur (M.S.) India.

Dr. J.F. Patil; Professor, United Western Bank, Late Shri R.N. Godbole Chair, Financial Management and Banking Research, Department of Commerce and Management Shivaji University, Kolhapur.

Dr. R.P. Kurulkar; (Retd.) Professor & Head Department of Economics, Dr. Babasaheb Ambedkar Marathwada University, Aurangabad; and Member, Marathwada Statutory Development Board, Aurangabad.

V.S. Kulkarni; Assitance General Manager, UWB.

Dr. K. Ramesha; National Insitute of Bank Management, Pune.

Dr. M. Narasimhulu; Professor & Head (Retd.), Principal Investigator, UGC. Major Research Project, Department of Economics, Osinamia University, Hyderabad.

A.A. Dange; Professor, Department of Economics, Shivaji University Kolhapur.

Dr. M.C. Kodli; Former Professor & Head, Department of Economics, Karnataka University, Dharwad.

1

VISION PLAN FOR AGRICULTRAL DEVELOPMENT OF WESTERN MAHARASHTRA

V.B. Jugale

PREAMBLE

It has been presumed by some of the experts that planning has no role to play in a market economy. Planning, in fact, has an inherent link with decision making processes of an individual or an enterprise or firm or an industry. Planning in a market economy can be visualised at the every state of competency in the system for example planning for a short period, long period and for perspective period as the case may be depending on the mission and goals of the firm, industry, enterprise or an individual.

In every economic system, whether it is a nation, organisation, institution, or an individual, dreams and visions are made with some action plans to realise them in near future. Hence there is no dearth of visionaries and thinkers in all economic systems. Development in all kinds of systems invariably require such kinds of visionaries and dreamers. Thinkers perceptively visualise the future dynamics. Accordingly the society can be awakened or prepare a mind setting of the public towards such dynamics can be reflected. Acceptability of a change was always the question of struggle for the visionaries. The gaps between present and future can be minimised or eliminated through visionary actions. The society or a system can be protected from the shapeless/baseless movements. So actionable blue print foreseeable in future can be earmarked for facing the dynamics. This will enable the system to set free from some rigid shackles which impede the progress at present. Shapping for the future density was enabled the thinkers to take lead in visionary actions.

An attempt has been made to formulate the visionary plan of agricultural development for Western Maharashtra during next two decades. Agrcitulture being a prime sector in India, what agenda is left to phase out the vision before the planners in fact is the main thrust of this paper.

TERMS AND REFERENCES

Agriculture, without any doubt is predominant in the Maharashtra State's economy in general and Western Maharashtra in particular. Notwithstanding the state's progress and the performance data on various aspects of the region's economy obviously replicated on the Maharashtra's significant facelift. In an intensively competitive global economy, the region cannot and must not afford to be complacent and rest on its past laurels and glory. It has to gear up to decisive action with long-term target and a vision to attain furthermore glory with sustainability.

At present the region is at a cross road and is passing through various odds and obstacles in agricultural growth. Soil salinity is caused by irrigation vis-à-vis monocrop-culture (by cultivating sugarcane) which has been the major agricultural disorder in the region. Besides growing typical diseases on sugarcane, soyabean is breaking the backbone of the agriculture sector in the regional economy. Huge investment poured on sugar industry and allied sectors is helpless and is unable to move round the wheels of industriousness. The real growth engines (sugar factories) repositioning the regional economy are in trouble. The W.T.O. challenges contracting the growth and discouraging the cooperative sector. The impressive performance of the sugar factories has been encountered by depressive and decisive role of the co-operators. The co-operator indeed are creators (promoters) and destroyers of the cooperative edifice. So many factors have been encountering to shrink the cooperative economy. To retain the laurels and glory of the region vision to thought off and the agenda to phase out the programme and to deal with the action plans is prioritised.

VISION STATEMENT AND OBJECTIVES

Vision statement is a sort of blue-print of the perspective plan strategy, which can be achieved with the prescribed dose of investment and technology. It is essential to carve out a vision for the state herself. Although the vision designed to be laid down with a mechanism to attain it as a part of administrative and policy matter. A vision statement must indicate a specific economic target to aspire for. The political needs can also be encountered in the vision statement, since its relevance to economic development is much more significant in the Indian context.

The State Government in October 2000 had circulated the "Second Discussion Draft" entitled "A Bold New Vision". Therein the state is desired to commit a strategy comprising the overwhelming thrust on physical infrastructure, services and social sectors along with some sectoral details.

The present vision plan and an agenda for agricultural development is centralised on the Western Maharashtra; a cluster of a few districts with specific geographical characteristics. It has the following objectives:

1. To highlight fundamental ground realities and the problems of agriculture in Western Maharashtra.
2. To work out for a vision plan of agriculture sector for and to phase out the Action Plans for the sectoral state efforts.
3. To recommend the Action Plan for agriculture development.
4. To identify the growth drivers.
5. To work out with a growth model for the integrated agricultural development in Western Maharashtra.

Thus the visionary statement and an agenda for the overall growth of agriculture and allied sector of Western Maharashtra is implied to have huge leap of quadrupling the state's present performance in various macro-economic variables, e.g., PCI, employment, investment, institutional networking, infrastructure, agro-industries, financial services, agricultural marketing, and filling up the gaps in sustained development etc.

The vision statement indicate a diversified and structural development processes rather than a mere growth in the present macro economic variables. The existing challenges, however can be converted into opportunities provided the humane face in respect of agricultural development is diversified by operationalising the agenda of economic reforms for perspective future growth of the region.

CHANGE IN MONSOON METEOROLOGY

The aggregate rainfall remaining the same, the dispersion of rainfall throughout the year is disturbing, devastating and causing damages to the crops grown in both ways i.e. heavy or scanty rainfall. The decrease in South-West monsoon and increase in post-monsoon rainfall no doubt has become a regular phenomenon. Consequently it is essential to change our crop planning for precision farming. The early sowing (during pre-monsoon period) of some crops like soyabean is now-a-days has become regular phenomenon. The sowing dates have to be adjusted as per the redefined rainfall period. Protective irrigation during the monsoon and protective crop measures during the post monsoon period has to be precisely confined. This confinement of cropping pattern should also requires to develop certain crop varieties suitable for Western agro-climatic zone of Maharashtra. Ratnagiri, Sindhudurga and Raigad which belongs to the Konkan zone and the eastern plateau of the Konkan consisting of Pune, Satara, Ahmednagar, Satara, Sangli, Kolhapur and Solapur require different cropping patterns. Better genotypes for rain resistance varieties for Konkan region and rainfed conditions in drought zone districts have to be emphasised. The drought tolerance cropping system has to be developed. The GM technology will work effectively in this regard. To take the benefit of heavy rainfall during the post monsoon period in drought area, proper topography based hydrological engineering abilities have to be applied to preserve or percolate the rain water into the grounds.

Village ponds, farm ponds, social forestry at the steep slopes, all types of bundings and majagies be developed. These programmes should be confined to the well planned watershed development programme and not for the implementation of Employment Guarantee Schemes or Sampurna Gramin Rojgar Yojana. These schemes are only targeted towards constructive works not the biological engineering activities. Proper planning from the edge to downstream of the watershed has to be integrated systematically.

PRECISION FARMING

Precision farming is the only alternative way out available to determine and decide on the cropping pattern congenial to the rainfall crop protection measures during the khariff and rubi seasons. The electronic revolution was spawned two technologies viz. GIS and GPS (Geographical Information System and Global Positioning System). Alongwith this, there is a wide range of sensors, monitors and controllers for agricultural equipments. Together, will enable the farmers to use such technologies for accurate and precise positioning and analyse all data in association with agronomic and climatic for powerful and progressive farm management. Precision farming should not be thought of as only yield mapping and variable rate fertiliser application and evaluated on only one or other. It will affect the entire production and management function of farm activities.

Use of remote sensing rainfall forecasting mechanism and astro-meteorology be developed and propagated throughout the region. An increased knowledge of all such technologies and information medias as per the need of the farming be developed in the region. The farmers should also initially know soil, hydrology, micro-climate and aerial photography. Following are some of elements of the precision farming:

1. Yield mapping
2. Variables rate fertilizer
3. Weed mapping
4. Variable spraying

5. Topography and boundaries
6. Salinity mapping
7. Guidance system
8. Records of analyses

Precision farming thus makes farm planning both easier and more complete. There is much more map data to utilise in determining long term cropping plans, erosion controls, salinity controls and assessment of tillage systems. Farmers have to work closer with several such professionals. These professionals shall be developed by the Government. A serious thought has to be given to the policy makers.

Similarly the weather based and crop based pest management techniques have to be taught to the farmers. Considering all the technicalities, it is essential to enhance all such requirements through Government organisations only. Private expertise will exploit the farmers.

FOUR PILLARS OF AGRICULTURAL AGENDA

M.S. Swaminathan Committee (2002) has rightly pointed out the important four pillars of future agricultural growth in Maharashtra viz. productivity, quality, profitability and sustainability. For which proper planning of agricultural resources with wider visions is highly essential. Land and water resources are the main concerns to agricultural productivity. The land and water use mapping with electronic links for achieving agricultural productivity has to be developed at the community level. Soil and salinity analysis has to be acknowledged to the farmers. The sugarcane yield in Western Maharashtra is declining due to mispriorities and mismanagement of agricultural land and water resources.

For improving the quality, due care has to be taken to increase the nutrient values of the agricultural yield. Quality revelation has to be enhanced through phytosanitary measures. The phyto-sanitary labs have to be developed by the state initiatives. The quality standards of different crops required for exports have to be made known to the farmers. Soil testing kits can be allotted through Government initiation.

Agriculture can be more profitable, if it is linked to non-farm activities and use of the yield for industrial processing.

Many times farmers use additional inputs than the required amount. This is unnecessary burden on them. Micro-entrepreneurial activities based on farm activities can be developed such as food processing, industry, hiring of farm equipments, repair centres, vermi-composting, agri-business centre, running laboratories, bio-mass, food parks, storage, commodity estates, e-commerce, animal husbandry, agri-clinics, etc.

Strengthening the ecological foundations for sustainable agricultural development is another area of economic reform. A livelihood basket including fruit, fodder, cereals, pulses, vegetables, spices, medicinal plants etc. is essential for healthy life style in India. Similarly, the State Government has also to witness for large amount of biomass from the grass on wasteland, fresh and composted leaves, .weeds from farms, crop wastes and glyricidia and other green manure crops along with an average of 2000 to 2500 litre of water per day from a nearby well or rivers, minimal equipment and financial support, training and motivation to the rural youths for the overall growth of the technological issues, conservation of biodiversity and biodiversity and bio-prospecting of wild species and valuable germplasm for bio-molecules and genes for commercialisation need to be documented at village and Panchayat levels as necessary part of the Biodiversity Act. Similar records of patents and rights of plant varieties and live stock have to be rights of plant varieties and live stock have to be maintained by developing genebanks. Ownership of geographical indication products like Kolhapur jaggery and chappals, Devagad alphanso, Paithani sarees have to be maintained.

Genetically modified crop/plant/animal technology plays a significant role in solving the food problem and other related problems in the economy. But it should be more consumer concern. Health, environment, loss of biodiversity cannot be denied in operationalising such technology in agriculture sector. It's pros and cons should be studied in detail.

WATER AND SOIL CONSERVATION

There are so many complexities in administering the solutions in respect of the adversities caused by soil conservation, management of irrigation water and salinity problems etc. In the drought zone, we are required to operationalise IWDPs along with water literacy. In the perennial irrigation area, particularly in sugarcane belt, we should be vary cautious about optimum water management techniques. At present more than 50,000 hectares of fertile cultivable land is affected by salinity in Sangli and Kolhapur districts. Soil erosion in Konkan and even in drought land area is becoming a serious problem due to unseasonal heavy rainfall. Encroachment of sea water in the uplands is another problem of salinity in Maharashtra. Proper steps towards the right directions are required to be taken for maintaining agricultural sustainability in the State. Implementation of integrated watershed development programmes in drought zone of the state is essential. The hydrological and ground water aquifer results are reflecting a positive response in the drought area. Similarly mismanagement in use of water resources in sugarcane belt has to be eliminated in to, for which water literacy programme along with multi-crop culture has to be undertaken widely in the perennial irrigated area. The incomplete irrigation projects particularly in Krishna basin have to be evolved for the optimum use of water resources.

Rainfall forecasting, temperature and humidity measurement equipments, capacity to analyse the risks in farm activities and to avoid the disasters and to create a competency in agri-business have to be enhanced as a major step for visionary development of agriculture in Maharashtra. Each and every farmer be able to diagnose the climatic change through electronic data base and also be made able to decide upon and to tackle the problems involved in it. Crop specific approaches based on the region specific is highly appreciable strategy to deal with visionary plans for development of agriculture sector. Low cost vis-à-vis high yielding technology be enchanced, for which research has to be emphasized at a large scale basis.

HORTICULTURE REVOLUTION

The state is considered as a horticulture state in India. The resource region of the Konkan is useful for developing the horticulture economy. Other district regions like Jalgaon, Pune, Sangli, Nasik, Solapur, Ahmednagar are very famous for growing banana, onion, grape, pomegranate etc. Considering the exposure to the global market, important changes in trade activities has to be undertaken immediately, in which commodities, complementarities and complexities have to be looked in prospectively. The state is not much attentive in agro-processing business as compared to industrial activities in general. Technology mission on horticulture that takes an integrated approach is needed. Lack of effective chain of cold storages is a major deterrent. The loss on account of water is also phenomenal. Air freight rates are higher and not encouraging compared to other countries. Lack of post-harvest facilities, inadequate certification and inability to build brands have conspired to keep farm produce of the world market. The EU norms be made favourable to us.

RESTRUCTURING AGRICULTURAL CREDIT SYSTEM

Restructuring of agricultural credit system is an agenda of reforms since two decade. Since the recommendations of the Khusro Committee, the issue is in concern with reformation congenial to the farm community. The existing system is generating burden of indebtedness. Credit worthiness is one of the traditional norm of loan borrowing. Now a day productivity is becoming an important indicator of credit worthiness. On the basis of which, the SHGs are growing. The need of micro-finances is the required input to micro-enterprises and for rural unemployed persons.

The Vaidhanathan Committee took a right direction to recommend a package of revival, which is compelled to accept it in to. Hence it is required to motivate the State Government to change their co-operative legislations. Simultaneously the RBI should also revive its banking regulation legislation. In principle, the report has been accepted by the Finance Minister.

The conversion of PACS into Co-operative Village Bank is my recommendation since last two decades. Its effectiveness has been tested in Kolhapur area. The results are encouraging. The conversion of PACS into CVBs is the best solution to the agricultural credit systems.

The three tier structure of the co-operative credit system required to be revived. The grassroot societies are experiencing the grass without roots. The upper organisations are operating at the graciousness of co-operation of the grassroot level societies. If the asset and liabilities of PACS are withdrawn from the upper institutions, the financial position of the upper agencies like DCCBs and SCBs will come to weaken their financial positions.

REVIVAL IN MARKETING SYSTEM

At present there are 28 legislations applicable to agricultural marketing. All these legislations have to be replaced by ideal marketing system. The regulated markets have to be scrapped and replaced by an alternative model. Marketing should be a beginning part of the agricultural activities prior to the agricultural production. The commercial intelligency in marketing activities should be developed and it should be trained in that direction. The import risk analysis, commodity oriented marketing approaches, marketing finance, post harvest technology for enhancing marketing efficiencies and increasing the producer's share in consumer rupee are some of the important subjects on the state reforms policies of the State Governments since decades.

Training the farmers in forward trading, contract farming and co-operate farming is now essential irrespective of the traditional attachment of land ownership. However, these attachments can be considered while developing a very useful system of marketing, beneficial to the farm community. The state's initiative in this direction is essential. Otherwise a common man will loose the faith on the Government. Farmers in distress and their suicides can only be eliminated by developing proper relief measures along with ideal insurance system. The micro insurance is a new idea introduced in the Budget 2005–06.

CONCLUDING REMARKS

The youth be attracted to the farm activities. The intelligent students should be attracted with some scholarships and fellowships to practice this core sector. The growth rate of agriculture sector as indicated in the National Agricultural Policy-2000 can only be achieved, if these issues are subjected to the agenda of economic reforms. The institutional commitments and responsibilities of the Government as a whole should be sustained by the State Government alone. The privatisation of such responsibilities and commitments can never exist. The state politics should be directed towards this end keeping in view the common man in the society. The co-operative sector should be revived and it should be freed from Government control step by step.

The trade related intellectual property rights in concern to farm and farmers, community patenting, strategic thinking on trade related activities have to be embarked. The farmers' and breeders' rights should be made known to the farmers by strategic campaigning.

REFERENCES

Jugale V.B. (1992), "Theories of Agricultural Finance", Atlantic Publishers, New Delhi.

Jugale V.B. (2204), "Horticulture Economy of Maharashtra", Shruti Publications, Jaipur.

Jugale V.B. (2003), "Towards Village Banking", Atlantic Publishers, New Delhi.

Jugale V.B. (2004), "Post-concern Agenda of Reforms for the SAARC Countries -6th IIDS Seminar", Colombo, November, 2004.

Government of Maharashtra (2003), "An Action Plan of Agriculture for Comming 25 Years (M.S. Swaminathan Committee Report)", MCAER, Pune.

MEDC (2000), Maharashtra Vision-2005" Fast Track Development of Maharashtra - Strategy and Action".

Government of Maharashtra -Agricultural Census Reports (1st and 2nd).

2

AGENDA FOR COOPERATION

Madhav V. Madane

BACKGROUND

Any Agenda for cooperation, meaning for Reforms in the Cooperative Way of Functioning, can best be drawn through a process of evolving a collective cooperative will formulated through a countrywide debate, on given issues, among constituents, mostly individuals,, of the Cooperative Movement. The Agenda, if drawn on the basis of a cooperative will, can best be in the form of guidelines for overall cooperative development within the broad framework of economic reform for the country. The ideal process for such evolution should be the expression of the cooperative will through a lobby of cooperators among the legislators and policy-makers. Care will have to be taken that such consensus for cooperative reforms must be within the limits of universal values, principles and practices recognised and observed for the development of a healthy Cooperative Movement.

THE SCOPE

Before initiating the process of Agenda formulation, care will have to be taken to ensure that knowingly or unwittingly, we do not venture to issue policy guidelines or legislate in matters which, if altered. Modified or removed could change the very character of the cooperative form of organization. Examples are not wanting of frequent pronouncements by policy-makers and arbitrary legislative and administrative measures which have drastically affected cooperative business practices and financial operations. The values and principles which have endured for over a century and the business ethics and practices which have stood the test of time, are worthy of respect and should receive due consideration for ensuring future integrity of our Cooperative Movement. It is important to note here that despite all the constraints, the Indian Cooperative Movement today is one of the largest movements in the world and according to the statistics of the International Cooperative Alliance (ICA), the Indian cooperatives have the largest number of individuals as their members.

21ST CENTURY OBJECTIVES

The Agenda for the Twenty first Century, or at least for the first quarter of it, should contain the broad objectives of the development strategy of future reform. The decades of trial and error and the present experimental approach must give way to a more rational, long-term as well a pragmatic statement of objectives backed by a realistic action programme for introducing legislative and administrative measures which will help restore to the cooperatives their right place in the national economy. While formulating such objectives and the work programme, the experience of the past Century in respect of government involvement in administrative and financial matters touching the business of cooperatives at various levels, should be taken into consideration. Reform pandits should also look back and examine it, in introducing the credit cooperatives in India, the Colonial Government did indeed intend to use the cooperative as a tool to control and regulate the socio-economic lives of the population in both rural and urban areas. Ignoring the past strategy of the pioneers and the experience of the past Century would only help perpetuate chaotic state of affairs in the matters concerning the cooperatives at all levels.

BRITISH LIBERALS AND THE INDIAN ELITE

Following the 1857 uprising and the rural unrest in late Nineteenth Century, the imperial lobby in England was desperately looking for a long-term solution to India's economic problems. A military solution was ruled out as impractical. In this situation, the liberals thought of a cooperative solution, but the consumer cooperatives in England were unsuitable for Indian conditions. Initiatives taken by Sir Horace Plunkett, who had considerable experience in the formation of Agricultural Banks in Ireland and Fourth Earl Grey, who had keen interest in cooperatives overseas, especially in India, narrowed down the choice, which could be suitable to India, to the type of rural cooperatives in Ireland, Germany and Italy. These liberals had around them a close circle of friends some of whom had experience of working in the Indian Civil Service. One of them was Lord Wenlock.

Lord Wenlock later became the Governor of Madras Province. He was the one who sponsored the mission of Sir Frederick Nicholson to study rural cooperatives in Europe and recommend suitable model for India.

We all know how Nicholson recommended Raiffeisen type agricultural cooperatives of Germany as the most suitable for Indian conditions; how the Edward Law Committee recommended enactment of suitable legislation and how the Indian Credit Cooperative Societies Act of 1904 was passed in the Governor General in Council in India. The creation of the post of a Registrar was recommended by Sir Henry Wolff who had considerable cooperative experience in England. Dr. Rita Rhodes, a cooperative researcher, in her recent study on Empire and Cooperatives, has in detail analysed these development. About the role of the Registrar in the Indian context, she has said, "India's early cooperative legislation of 1904 and 1912 took the role of the colonial cooperative registrar far beyond that of his British counterpart and created a model for subsequent colonial cooperative development."

The 1904 Act was essentially a piece of enabling legislation. While piloting the Bill, the authors of the proposal made it clear that the Act is intended "to encourage thrift, self-help and cooperation amongst agriculturists, artisans and persons of limited means." It was explained that, it was for the people to decide if they would like to form the cooperatives; only the guidance would be given by officials. Later on Registrars and officials like Calvert, J. McNeil, C.S. Campbell, Sir Malcolm Darling, and C.F. Strickland effectively played the role of a Friend, Philosopher and Guide. Campbell, who was a keen writer had in one of his diaries stated, "The Registrar himself, of course, has to be most careful not to erect a tripod which falls to the ground when his two feet are removed, but he has no objection to nursing an infant society till it can stand on its own legs." Campbell was also of the view that guidance can be given by officials or non-officials; it does not matter. These officials shied away from a control mechanism; and provided a kind of Official Leadership to the Movement.

Most of the cooperatives, started during the initial years in the Bombay Province, were established by non-official leaders who were active in educational and socio-economic institutions. Some of these cooperatives, such as the Cosmos Cooperative Bank and the Shamrao Vithal Cooperative Bank, as well as many cooperatives at different levels, are already in their Centenary Year and many others would follow soon. They have put before us a model which succeeded without government help and guidance. On the other hand, many cooperatives in credit, marketing, processing and several other sectors, despite Government assistance, have failed to deliver goods and are incurring losses from year to year.

THE MARBURG STATEMENT

During September 1904, at the initiative of the Marburg University in Germany, a Colloquium was held to debate on 100 Years Cooperative Credit Societies Act, India. 1904. The Colloquium was titled: "Classical British-Indian Pattern of Cooperation" from State Partnership to State Control. It was described as "A Worldwide Applied Model of Cooperative Legislation. Experts from countries as far away as Canada, Australia, Africa, United kingdom, UN/ ILO, myself from India and Finland participated. All of us debated on the impact of the 1904 Act in different parts of the world, due to the British colonial link. It was astonishing to hear the replication of the credit societies model, in different forms and under varying nomenclature, in different parts of the World. Logically the State association and the role of the Registrar were the topics widely debated upon. I am reproducing below the relevant two paragraphs of the executive summary concerning State and Cooperation in the concerned countries in general and India in particular.

What was initially planned as state-sponsorship of member-oriented self-help organizations, tended to turn into state-control of local organizations serving mainly the interests of the State. This had far-reaching effects on cooperative legislation with wide margins of discretion turning into a detailed, rigid, bureaucratic and coercive legal framework.

"Gradually it is rediscovered that cooperatives work best when left to operate according to their own rules and principles. It is realized that in the long run no government can afford to finance a huge bureaucracy of cooperative officers, supervisors, inspectors and auditors and that the main advantage of promoting cooperative development is defeated, if cooperatives fail to mobilize and pool their members' own resources but rather depend on government or other external support." Following are some of the main areas which should be given priority on the Reform Agenda for Cooperation. I wish to emphasize that these recommendations are not addressed only to the Government but all concerned with functioning of our cooperatives.

RESTORATION OF AUTONOMY

The top priority on the Agenda for Cooperative Reform, therefore, will have to be given to reversing the present trend of centralization of powers in the hands of the State, under various provisions of Cooperative Laws, should begin in the near future. This will help bring the cooperatives at par with other sectors of our economy in accordance with the present national policy of liberalization and de-regulation. The latest announcement of the government to give maximum autonomy to public sector undertakings is indicative of the government's intentions to free all sectors from State control. In contrast to public sector enterprises, the cooperatives are autonomous institutions, formed and run by members. They should be the first to qualify for self-regulation and to be freed from State control. There are elaborate provisions in all our National Laws to regulate all kinds of economic and financial transactions of public institutions. The arbitrary powers of Government and the Cooperative Departments have no place in the present climate of globalization and de-regulation.

During the post-independence decades, the relations between cooperatives and the government were strengthened in several ways. Recommendations of various committees, especially the All-India Rural Credit Survey Committee, resulted in increased government and Reserve Bank of India participation in matters relating to cooperative finance and management. The recommendations of the Gorwala Committee resulted in direct participation in equity capital and management. With the result that the decision-making process gradually shifted from the hands of representative management to the government departments and central financing institutions. Cooperative Laws became more elaborate and coercive. Ironically, majority of the cooperatives, which were self-governed and autonomous during the pre-independence period, lost their freedom to govern themselves.

LEGISLATIVE REFORMS

The process of legislative reform should get precedence in the Reform Agenda. The pre-independence Preamble, which was replaced to convert the cooperatives as instruments for implementing planned development, in accordance with the Directive Principles of the Constitution, should be restored to give the cooperatives their rightful place as institutions for the promotion of thrift, self-help, and mutual cooperation among people of common economic needs. The legislation should hereafter be in the form enabling Laws with provisions which will facilitate cooperative functioning on democratic lines. The powers given to the State in post-independence period are no longer relevant in the policy framework of the Twenty first Century. In addition, these legal provisions are repugnant to the universally accepted values and principles of the Cooperative Movement. This will enable the Registrar to function in future as a Friend, Philosopher and a Guide of the cooperatives and not their Creator, Preserver and Destroyer.

COOP. MINISTERS' CONFERENCES

In the Asia-Pacific Region, Cooperative Ministers' Conferences are held at periodic intervals under the auspices of the Regional Office of the International Cooperative Alliance (ICA) for this Region. These Conferences issue recommendations to the governments and cooperative movements in the Region to Streamline their cooperative policies and legislation. Few of these recommendations are put into practice. Many of them, if implemented, can have a very positive impact on cooperative development in the Region. Sadly, most of the measures suggested remain on paper.

In the summary of country paper presented by India at the 6th Ministers' Conference held at Kathmandu from 3rd to 6th April 2002, it was stated, "National Policy on Cooperatives has been put in place to facilitate all round development of cooperatives in the country. Under this policy cooperatives would be provided necessary legislative and policy support and assistance to enable them to work as autonomous, self-reliant and democratically managed institutions accountable to their members." To ensure this, the first important step is to withdraw all powers given to Heads and senior officers of the Cooperative Department to suspend elected boards, take over cooperative managements, cancel or disapprove decisions taken by a general body or the managing committees, which are within the limits of their authority, and powers to approve or disapprove expenditures or disbursal of funds of legitimate purposes and within the scope of objectives of such cooperatives. We do not see any substantial move in the country in that direction.

Once the legislative reforms come into effect, the cooperatives would be able to breathe freely, would be able to plan and implement their policies and programmes in accordance with the collective will of the members as democratically expressed in the general body meetings. Even if most of the control mechanism, set up under present legislative measures, there are enough powers in the hands of the government to remedy any situation under different laws and regulations. Once the legal framework becomes conducive to free cooperative growth, most of the top-heavy departments would be redundant within a short span of time.

ENSURING FINANCIAL DISCIPLINE

One of the most disturbing aspects of cooperative finance today is the total lack of discipline in respect of resource mobilization and disbursal of funds and utilization of allotted resources for the purposes for which they have been mobilized. The credit cycle is almost on the verge of collapse and frequent State intervention makes the matter from bad to worse. Too many players in the field of finance does not allow the credit cycle to function smoothly and the variable factors tempt both the lenders and the borrowers to seek easy solutions to the most complicated problems. There is total confusion and mix-up over obligation to return borrowed money, relief measures under crop failure and drought, government assistance in disaster affected zones and waiver by Government in respect of repayment of loans from lending agencies.

At the Third Regional Cooperative Forum, held under the auspices of the International Cooperative Alliance-Asia Pacific, at Chieng Mai in Thailand during the first week of December 2004, Mr. YSP Thorat, Managing Director of the National Bank for Agriculture and Rural Development (India) was invited to address the Forum. The theme of the Forum was "Re-engineering Cooperatives in a Global Economy". Speaking on 'Re-engineering Cooperative Banks in India' Mr. Thorat dwelt up the qualitative Impairment in the functioning cooperative banks under four heads. viz., 1. Financial impairment; 2. governance impairment; 3. Management impairment; and 4. Regulatory impasse. As regards financial impairment, Mr. Thorat stated: "(a) Nearly half the retail outlets at the ground level are loss-making cooperatives; (b) As on 31st March 2004, around 20% of provincial banks and around 40% of sub-provincial banks were not having the minimum capital requirement stipulated by the Central Bank; (c) The gross accumulated losses of the system are around 110 Billion and distributed roughly equally between the primary agricultural credit societies and the sub provincial cooperative banks; and (d) the cooperative credit structure accepts public deposits in addition to members deposits. Supervisory findings reveal erosion of public deposits to the extent of Rs. 3 Billion at the sub provincial and provincial cooperative banks."

This confusion does not allow flow of funds in the normally accepted pattern. Because of increasing percentage of over-dues, financing agencies like NABARD, are looking for other institutions, such as Self-help Groups (SHG's), to channel their funds for productive purposes. The scope of finance through this channel is extremely limited because in this process, the NGOs have to play the role an important part in maintaining credit worthiness of the borrowings SHGs. Mr. Thorat has suggested, "In view of the significant impairment of the cooperative credit structure necessitating immediate reform the question arises as to whether a re-engineering framework can be devised within an implementable action plan." In my opinion, the following measures are needed to be taken to streamline financial activities and restore solvency to the cooperative societies.

(a) Phased Withdrawal of Government Capital: A time bound schedule is needed to be prepared to phase out Government Share Capital from all types of Cooperatives.

(b) Waiver of loans given by cooperatives should be avoided. If absolutely essential, after a careful scrutiny, the cooperatives should be compensated to the extent of the amount of losses suffered by them or their members.

(c) Loan recovery procedures should be simplified and as far as possible, the repayment should be linked to other business transactions between the society and the members.

(d) Under no circumstances, governments should provide funds for losses and misapplication of funds due to corruption or mismanagement in cooperative financial and business transactions;

(e) A percentage of savings by members to their total transactions with the society should be made obligatory; and

(f) Statutory audit should be retained with the Government.

MONITORING AUTHORITY

An independent Authority to monitor business and financial transactions of all cooperatives should be established. This Authority should have officials from the Cooperative Departments and the Reserve Bank of India. The Monitoring Authority should function as an Independent Wing in the Ministry of Finance in each State. Following should be the main functions of the Authority.

1. To examine and Interpret Audit Reports: This work should be done in accordance with the objectives and the bye-laws of each cooperative and to see if action has been taken on the Audit Report. If not to recommend suitable measures;
2. To Interpret the Balance Sheet to see if the same reflects the true financial condition of the said society. If necessary to correct the situation by recasting the Balance Sheet and related documents accordingly, and return them to the concerned society for necessary action.
3. To examine if fictitious transactions are used to show loan recovery and issue of fresh loans to the borrowers to demonstrate greater percentage of loan recovery; and
4. The Authority should have the power and discretion, where necessary, to set things right by advice and assistance before recommending any action against the concerned society. For this purpose, the Authority should use the government departmental field staff for cooperatives at various levels.

THE DEVELOPMENT DECADES

To counter the effect of reduced government financial and managerial assistance, cooperatives should declare the next two decades as Development Decades. The shift in emphasis in cooperative operations should be from over dependency on external sources of working capital, re-examination of the resource base by involving the members and reorganizing the management on the basis of accepted business standards. The field staff of the Cooperative Department should play an important role in guiding the cooperatives in the reorganization process. Simultaneous efforts will need to be initiated to strengthen business and organizational relations between the primaries and their federations and apex level institutions. Optimum utilization of the resources, expertise, man-power, operational and managerial experiences of all cooperatives should be pooled and put to use to mutual advantage. Mutuality of interests among the cooperatives will avoid duplication of effort and maximize use of available resources and expertise. This will also help cooperatives with limited means to come out of their shell and work towards a viable status. The parameters of cooperative viability will have to be accurately defined. In the debate on Cooperative Viability at the recent Annual National Convention of the Indian Society for Studies in Cooperation (ISSC), the Report of the Technical Session - II, as summarized by Prof. V.D. Jugale had stated, "Cooperative Viability is a customer Centric approach, whereas Economic Viability is business centric approach."

Integrated Services

The present march of our economy towards globalization has created many difficulties and handicaps for our small and medium business and economic units; but at the same time it has opened up before them a wide world of opportunities in several directions. A look at the present scenario, including in areas relating to finance, trade in farm products, easy availability of bank finance, improved technology for cultivation, processing, transportation, communication and access to many other facilities, gives the cooperatives vast dimension and scope of opportunities waiting to be exploited.

To obtain maximum advantage of the opportunities before us, the cooperatives should aim at building integrated services from planning, production and marketing to bring back to their members maximum returns for their products and services. In this process, the federations at all levels can help obtain for the primary members, speedy market information in terms in respect of price structure for various commodities, quality in demand in different markets, the buyers and exporters of the products we wish to buy in return and the most important information on our competitors.

Many will wonder how this is possible in our country. I would like to state that there is no miracle involved in this activity. It is the result of hard work, planning, optimum utlilization of resources. Let us take an example.

The average farm holding in Japan is less than a hectare. But with the help of their cooperatives, the farmer members of agricultural cooperatives are able to obtain adequate income which meets all their production and living costs and also helps them save from year to year. The planning is done with the help of farm guidance advisers (same as our extension staff. The planning takes into account not only farm production needs, but also the costs for family expenses on education, health, social activities and needed savings. The crop pattern is decided with the guidance of farm advisers by using the results of government experimental farms. Quite often, these small plots of land are further divided into small lots for different crops. Advance market information, on a continuing basis, plays an important part in sending the products to the most profitable sales outlet. Right product to the right market is the motto. the result is that currently, majority of Japanese farmers have enough savings and their deposits often exceed the loans they may take from their cooperatives.

Decentralised Planning and Viability

While working towards de-regulation, the cooperatives, under the guidance of their federations, will have to try to integrate various services by pooling the resources and attaining economies of scale. However, the planning should begin at the primary level on the basis of an agreed pattern. The aim should be viability at each stage. Integrated services will lose their advantage if certain units in the total chain of operations lose their viability. Planning at the base level will be more realistic, will be in tune with local socio-economic conditions and will help reflect in the total plan, the actual requirements of production capital as well as input or raw material needs and commodity as well as financial surpluses from the integrated planned area.

SOCIAL INTEGRATION

Cooperatives are often accused of functioning in isolation of the community in which they operate. This is a worldwide phenomenon. In a country like India, where the economy is dominated by agriculture and its vulnerability to vagaries of nature. The addition of the Seventh Principle of Community and Cooperation was made to ICA's latest revision of Cooperative Principles keeping in mind this particular aspect of cooperative functioning. The cooperatives hereafter should take more interest in the problems of the community surrounding them by joining in local health, hygiene, education and employment generation activities. They can also effectively take part in creating infrastructure and running local transport and communication services to mutual benefit. We already have very good examples of cooperatives in setting up such services in several parts of the country, more particularly in the Western parts of the country and remarkably in Kolhapur and its surroundings. This ensures acceptability by the community of the cooperatives and their services.

Social Audit

With the possibility of widening the scope of cooperative activity, it is essential to add social dimension to cooperative audit, Social audit enables the members and the community to understand and interpret the objectives and impact of each cooperative activity. In several countries and in some places in India, social audit is being included on a selective basis. We should aim at introduction of social audit in phased manner.

AGENDA-A PARTICIPATORY PROCESS

The task of formulating the Agenda for Cooperative Reform should no more be limited to Government secretariats, cooperative departments and to boards of banking institutions. It should become the concern of all cooperatives and their members assisted by experts from all above institutions and departments. The Cooperative Will, formulated on the basis a countrywide issue related debates and technical surveys, should prevail. We have to be realistic and learn from our failures and wrong strategies. Most of our current cooperative problems are the result of availability of easy money, laxity of supervision and control mechanism, overbearing presence of Government personnel, close proximity of political parties and lack of understanding of obligations towards the society and fellow members.

As has been emphasized in the ICA's Identity Statement, "The values of self-help and self-responsibility accentuate the need for individual commitment and the centrality of the member experience. Democracy, when effectively implemented, allows for the voicing of different views, opportunity for discussions, and a way of resolving differences. A commitment to equity and equality reduces possibilities for exploitation form within and without cooperatives and encourage the pursuit of collective as well as individual interest, as does the emphasis on solidarity."

It is futile to persist in perpetuating the same system of experimenting at the cost of cooperatives and their members from decades to decades. Pioneers of the Cooperative Movement in India have worked very hard to establish and nourish the cooperatives and left behind a legacy of creativity and diligence. If we remember their contribution and the values they practiced, we have very good chance to overcome our present day problems and handicaps. A Cooperative Movement, which has survived, progressed and has shown remarkable results in several fields of our economy during its First Century, has every chance of continuity during the Second Century and beyond as also increasing its capability for serving the rural as also the urban communities in different parts of the country.

REFERENCES

Indian Cooperative Movement: A Profile. Vision 2005. NCUI.

British Liberalism and Indian Cooperation. Dr. Rita Rhodes. Open University, Walton Hall, (UK). Paper read at the Marburg University Colloquium. Germany.

Re-engineering Cooperative Banks in India. Mr. YSP Thorat, Managing Director, NABARD. Paper read at ICA Regional Forum, Chieng Mai, Thailand.

Why Cooperate in a Competitive World. Prof. Ian MacPherson, University of Victoria, Canada.

Colonial Cooperatives through the eyes of their Coop. Registers: Dr. Rita Rhodes, Research paper read at the Conference of the University of Valencia.

Report of the Technical Session-II IISC Convention, on Cooperative Viability, Prof. V.B. Jugale, Shivaji University, Kolhapur.

A Century of Indian Cooperatives. Chapter in Robert Owen Society Publication, Tokyo Japan.

Agricultural Cooperatives in Japan; the Dynamics of their Development, M.V. Madane, ICA Asia-Pacific, New Delhi.

Colloquium on Hundred Years Cooperative Credit Societies Act. India 1904. A Worldwide Applied Model of Cooperative Legislation. Prof. Hans-H Muenkner, Marburg University, Germany.

Executive Summary of the Colloquium. Prof. Hans-H Muenkner.

3

AGENDA OF AGRICULTURAL AND CO-OPERATIVE SECTOR REFORMS FOR THE STATES IN INDIA

R.R. Doshi

1. The economic reforms programme since 1991 till this day has not touched directly the following two sectors:

   (a) agriculture } No reforms for these sectors
   (b) cooperatives }

   Reason?: Reforms in the nodal sectors of the economy—trade sectors, industries sector and financial sector—which were more significant in the globalisation framework, would, by themselves promote reforms in these two vital sectors also: approach.

2. But now,: Since May 22, 2004, with assuming of power by the present government, agricultural development is being brought in the forefront as 'engine of overall economic growth.' However, so far, there is no specific agenda for the agricultural sector. Agenda for the cooperative sector appears to be out of sight.

PROBABILITIES

Can we consider either or both of the following two as facets of Agricultural Sector Reforms Agenda?

1. New Agricultural Policy, 2000
2. Proposals for agricultural sector in the Union Budgets, 2004–05 and 2005–06.

Answer: No. They are discrete proposals and not an integrated package of an agenda.

AGRICULTURE: ISSUES AT STAKE

- Increase in production through productivity increase
  - Need for 'productivity revolution'.
- Sustainable agriculture, for which:
  - (a) Need to avoid land degradation by any reason
  - (b) Rain water harvesting;
  - (c) Emphasis on water-shed development work
  - (d) Extending production of pulses and oilseeds in dry-land areas.
  - (e) Avoiding monoculture; following crop rotation.
- Use of new technology: 'Eco-Regional Technology Mission' to be launched.
- Increase in agricultural incomes through:
  1. Crop insurance
  2. Post-harvest technology
  3. Efficient institutional support
  4. Generating new employment opportunities
  5. Water management
  6. Land use planning.
- Creation of new employment opportunities through:
  1. Livestock and tree farming.
  2. Horticultural development with particular attending to post-harvest technology.
  3. Fisheries, coastal forestry (agro-forestry) and integrated crop and animal husbandry.
  4. Value-addition industrial activities.

- Institutional support
    1. Efficient marketing systems
    2. Credit institutions
    3. Processing units: linkage with credit and marketing
    4. Information system: Internet connected Rural Knowledge Centres gradually owned and operated by farmers themselves.
- Briefly, the agenda should be based on
    1. Removal of controls and distortions
    2. Providing of incentives and support institutions.

AGENDA FOR COOPERATIVE

- Core Areas for Co-operatives:

  • Credit • Marketing • Processing

  input supplies including irrigation: consumer.
- Operational efficiency and economic viability.
- Service to the maximum number as members.
- Big size of operation.
- Use of information technology.
- Modern systems of management.
- Least possible political intervention.
- Financial responsibility and efficiency by the leaders.
- Structural overhauling.
- Government support without undue controls.
- Accounting transparency and honesty.

4

IRRIGATION REFORMS IN MAHARASHTRA

S. G. Bhogle

INTRODUCTION

Water is a precious natural resource, but a limited one. It is a basic human need as well as inevitable for development. The growing population, industrialization and over all development has made this limited resource scare. Also there is uneven distribution of water resources throughout the state making it more challengable.

At the World Food Summit in 1996, the Food and Agriculture Organisation (FAO) estimated that 60 per cent of the extra food required must in future come from irrigated agriculture. The International Commission on Irrigation and Drainage (ICID) estimated that current food production would have to double within the next 25 years. The ICID strategy for implementing the Vision for Water for Food refers to the same FAO estimate regarding the role of irrigated agiculture in sustaining future world food supplies. The new slogan **"more crop per drop"** crystallizes the objective to be achieved by ICID member countries, particularly those that have nearly reached full development of their scarce water resources. (IPTRID Issue p. 4, 2003).

During last three years, irrigation has been high on political agenda in Maharashtra. In particular there has been a focus on improving water use efficiency, reducing water losses in irrigation and supplying water for non-irrigation purposes. To tackle these problems, water should be used efficiently and econommically. To achieve this goal, there is a need to make best use of advanced technology and management techniques.

BENCHMARKING

Benchmarking can be defined as:

> "A systematic process for securing continual improvement through comparison with relevant and achievable internal or external norms and standards".

The overall aim of benchmarking is to improve the performance of an organization as measured against its mission and objectives. Benchmarking implies comparison—either internally with previous performance and desired future targets, or externally against similar organization, or organizations performing similar functions. Benchmarking is a management tool already in use in both the public and private sector organisations.

On this background let us review a few important highlights as well as reforms in the irrigation sector.

HIGHLIGHTS OF WATER RESOURCES DEPARTMENT

Irrigation Department has been now renamed as Water Resources Department. This is in tune with the name of Ministry of Water Resources (MOWR) at Central Government. Today the subject of water is tackled in Maharashtra by Irrigation Department, Command Area Development, Maharashtra Jeevan Pradhikaran, GSDA, Rural Development Department through Zilla Parishads, Water Conservation Department etc. It is expected that the subject of water should be dealt holistically and its planning and use should be done in an integrated manner. Renaming of Irrigation Department in Maharashtra is a first step towards this overall change.

The Water Resources Department (till recently known as Irrigation Department) in Maharashtra has got several highlights which makes it a progressive and distinguished Water Resources Department compared with irrigation or similar department of other States in India. Some of these highlights are discussed below.

(i) *CADAs:* The work of Command Area Development Authorities (CADAs) has been effectively done in Maharashtra under Centrally sponsored CAD programme of Ministry of Water Resources (MOWR), GOI.

(ii) *WALMI, Aurangabad:* Water And Land Management Institute (WALMI), situated at Aurangabad in Maharashtra is celebrating its 25th Anniversary year. This Institute has done excellent work in imparting in-service training to the officers of Irrigation & Agriculture Departments and Farmers, Women Farmers, NGO Workers *etc.* during last 24 years and is recognised as one of the Premier Training Institutes in the country.

(iii) *Dam Safety Organisation:* There is an independent Dam Safety Organisation at Nasik started by Irrigation Department of the Government of Maharashtra and Dam safety Act is under the process of approval.

(iv) *Central Designs Organisation (CDO):* A Central Designs Organisation (CDO) is functional as a separate unit of Irrigation Department at Nasik looking after the designs of dams and major structures.

(v) *Directorate of Irrigation Research & Development (DIRD):* Directorate of Irrigation Research & Development at Pune is a unique organisation of ID of Govt. of Maharashtra which is incharge of Irrigation Research & Development, Design & execution of drainage schemes. It also publishes a quarterly magazine in Marathi, viz. Sinchan, dedicated to the water sector.

(vi) *Dr. Chitale Commission:* The Government of Maharashtra is studying carefully the report submitted by the Second Water & Irrigation Commission headed by Dr. M.A. Chitale, and is implementing several reforms recommended by the Commission.

IMPORTANT REFORMS

Let us briefly review some of the important reforms implemented/ in the process of implementation initiated by Water Resources Department, GOM.

(a) *State Water Policy:* As decided in the National Water Policy 2002, the Maharashtra state water policy has been adopted in July 2003 with objective of ensuring sustainable development and optimal use and management of the State's Water Resources to provide the greatest economic and social benefit for the people of the State. It has been published and is available on the web site of GOM (www. mahagovid.org.)

(b) *Maharashtra Water Resources Regulatory Authority (MWRRA):* Maharashtra Water Resources Regulatory Authority bill has been in the state Assembly in Dec. 2004. The Bill is sent to Joint Legislative Committee for scrutiny. The Authority will regulate sectoral allocation, water rates, changes in water use/ diversion of water use and compensation for such changes in water use. The draft is available on the above mentioned web site.

(c) *Maharashtra Management of Irrigation Systems by Farmers (MMISF Act):* The act is stand-alone act which will strengthen further the operation of Water Users Associations in the state. The bill is currently being scrutinized by the Joint Legislative Committee.

(d) *Irrigation Act 1976 Revision & Rules:* Revision of Irrigation Act 1976 & rules thereunder is in process.

(e) *Publishing of Irrigation Status Reports:* Water Resources Department, Govt. of Maharashtra is publishing the annual status report since 2002–2003 & the report for the year 2003–2004 is also published in Sept. 2004. This is an important official document highlighting important aspects of the functioning and performance of the Department providing up-to-date information about creation of irrigation potential, water availability, water use, water use efficiency, cropped area & crop yields, assessment & recovery *etc.* for all projects in the state.

(f) *Water Audit:* To improve water use efficiency, water audit has been made compulsory. The regulatory framework is set up for effective implementation of water auditing the irrigation projects throughout the state. The accountability for efficient utilisation of the project is fixed on the officer responsible for irrigation management.

(g) *On Farm Development Manual:* On Farm Development Manual (1982) is revised in Nov. 2003.

The salient features of this proposed Act are presented below in a synoptic style.

MAHARASHTRA MANAGEMENT OF IRRIGATION SYSTEMS BY FARMERS ACT, 2003 (MMISF ACT, 2003)

It is proposed to briefly present one of the major reforms in Irrigation sector, viz. MMISF Act 2003.

Objectives

- To bridge the gap between Irrigation Potential created actual Utilisation.
- To use water Equitably & Efficiently.
- To instill amongst farmers a sense of ownership of project & water.
- To hand over M & R and Management of Canals of WUAs to achieve:
  - Increase in quality
  - Appropriate use of funds
  - Decrease dependence on Govt.
  - Downsize Govt's administration
  - Achieve significant reduction in Govt. expenditure
  - Obtain help from International organizations
  - Streamline water management

Process

- Transparency & Peoples Participation.
  - Draft of the Act discussed at special Seminars at six regional HQs in the State
  - Interested persons, Institutions, NGOs and People's representatives purposefully involved in Seminars & discussions.

- Appropriate suggestions accepted & Draft changed accordingly.
- People Participation Act through Peoples Participation!

Approach

- Slow but steady
- Change with continuity
- From bottom to top
    - First, WUAs at Minor Level (Primary Unit)
    - Then upper level WUAs
- Stand alone Act
    - Registration, Agreements, etc. with Irrigation Department (ID) only
    - Support, supervision, Techno-managerial guidance,
    - Control & Monitoring to be done by ID only.
- Compatible with Techno-Socio-Economic changes world over

  Explicit provisions for:
    - Volumetric supply of water to WUAs.
    - Freedom of cropping.
    - Freedom of recycling water and conjuctive use of surface and ground water.
    - Equitable distribution.
    - Separate Chapter for Lift Irrigation.
- Conceptual clarity
    - Water quota defined.
    - Strategy during shortage of water explained.
    - Linkages with non-irrigation demands identified.

Comprehensive/Interdisciplinary Provisions for Providing Strong Foundation to PIM

- Engineering:
    - Joint Inspection, Repairs, Rehabilitation &

- Handing over of Management to WUA.
- Installation of measuring devices.
- Water budgeting.
- Functions of WUA & appropriate Authority spelt out.

• Socio-Economic

- Constitution of WUAs at various levels in phased/gradual manner.
- Election of Chairpersons & Members of Managing Committee.
- Sources & Utilisation of funds.
- Conflict Resolution/Appeals.

• Legal

- Delineation of WUAs at various levels.
- Agreement with WUA.
- Powers given to WUAs.
- Offences & Penalties.
- Recovery of water charges.
- Act applicable to existing to WUAs.

• Administrative

- Resignation, disqualification... Dissolution.
- Authentication.
- Removal of difficulties.
- Rules.

Rules under above-mentioned Act are also being drafted

Initiative taken by Water Resources Department of Govt. of Maharashtra in introducing various reforms is commendable. Such innovative reforms coupled with dedicated bureaucracy & active involvement and participation of all stakeholders will indeed bring about blue revolution in our state, which is the need of the time.

5

AGRICULTRUAL DEVELOPMENT: LIMITATIONS OF CREDIT

A.R. Padoshi

INTRODUCTION

The present paper is an attempt to understand the role and the limitations of credit to transform a traditional agriculture into a modern one. The paper has five sections. We begin by discussing the theoretical aspects of credit as a means of agricutlural development.

AGRICULTURAL CREDIT: THEORETICAL POINTS

Credit plays an extremely important role in the transformation of a traditional agricultural setup. Provision of adequate and timely credit facilitates capital flow[1] in agriculture. Credit also enables the farmer to have a wider choice of inputs and thus helps him to vary the input mix which is critically important for agricultural development.

The agrarian structure of most of the developing countries is characterized by a large number of small farmers and India is no exception. The percentage of small farmers in the Indian Context is easily over 75 most of the small cultivators are resource poor and they badly need the modernization of their farms at the earliest. It is in this context that credit assumes a crucial importance. Unless adequate and timely credit is made available to the small farmers and that to at a lower (subsidized) rate of interest modernization of agriculture in general and small farms in particular would not take place. Transformation or modernization of (especially) small farms is essential (at least in India) to mitigate to a great extent the problem of poverty and unemployment. Credit becomes a pre conditioned for agrarian modernization in an over populated and developing country like Inida.

Credit becomes essential in a traditional and under developed agricultural set-up from another angle. By its very nature agricultural production in seasonal. This seasonality is even more pronounced in a traditional agriculture due to limited extent of double cropping. In other words the process of income generation is seasonal for a traditional cultivator. But the consumption (by the cultivators family) is NOT a seasonal activity. Owing to the generally low level of their income, the farmers in the traditional agriculture need credit to finance their consumption also during the off season. Thus "In a traditional agriculture, problems of finance and credit arise in large part from a seasonal cycle of production which is super imposed on a largely non-seasonal or steady pattern of total consumption."[2]

Necessity of credit to the farmers arises at the time of repayment also. From the view point of repayment discipline, the loan should be repaid by the borrower well in time. However, many times, due to the inherent instability[3] of agriculture, especially in the traditional agriculture set-up, the cultivators find it extremely difficult to repay the loan along with the interest. Here credit becomes necessary (by means of re-scheduling etc. the loans) to help the farmers to tide over this difficulty.

Nevertheless, an important observation must be remembered when we discuss the contribution of credit or finance to transform or modernize a traditional agrarian set-up. The observation is that the credit would be successful in transforming traditional agriculture provided it helps those (farmers) who have potentially adequate economic base. Because, credit on an uneconomic basis—or on a basis which does not have adequate potential—becomes a GRANT. Such grants may destroy the repayment discipline and thus undermine the very strength of the credit institutions themselves[4].

Thus, in the case of agriculture, timely credit becomes essential not only for the purpose of production (and marketing), But also for consumption and repayment purposes.

In the next section viz. section III we examine the empirical data about the efforts made in India to extent adequate credit to the farmers in India.

AGRICULTURAL CREDIT: THE EMPIRICAL PICTURE

The provision of agricultural credit in India has been, almost wholly, government initiated and government sxponsored[5]. The government has been fixing the targets for agricultural credit and exhorting the public sector banks (PSB), regional rural banks (RRB), co-operatives (Co-op) and off course the NABARD, to fulfill the targets by making available to the farmers the amount of credit fixed by the Govt. as the target for the years. We will note only the recent data in this context. Thus, for the year 2003–04 the target of agricultural credit was Rs. 80,000/- crores. In July 2004 the target was fixed as Rs. 1,05,000/- crores for 2004–05 which was raised to Rs. 1,08,500/- crores for 2004–05. The Finance Minister in July 2004 promised the doubling of agricultural credit in three credit in three years.[6] The target for the coming financial year viz. 2005–06 the target becomes a little more than Rs. 1,41,000 crores. Every year the target has to be 30 per cent more than the target for its previous year.[7] In addition, the Finance Minister has also exhorted the various credit agencies to increase the number of borrowers by at least 50 lakhs (i.e., 50 lakh new names) every year. Clearly, the objective of the Govt. is to increase the amount of credit and also ensure that the credit facilities are adequately diffused over a larger number of farmers and not remain concentrated among a smaller number. Thus the objective is quite laudable.

The topic of agricultural credit has been a subject of study and research by many researchers, institutions and, of course, by Committees. Ever since 1954 (All India Rural Credit Survey Committee: RCS) there has been a production of volumes and volumes of studies, analyses and a plethora of suggestions and recommendations, all of which have been quite valuable. Recently, Rakesh Mohan (RM)[8] has written a scholarly and highly informative article about agricultural credit in India. Thus according to RM the percentage of agricultural credit to agricultural GDP has risen from a meagre 0.5 per cent (1950–51) to 8.7 per cent in 2001–02. But agricultural credit as a percentage of total credit in the country has been declining. The article also notes that the share of the institutional sources in the total agricultural credit has risen from 31.7 per cent in 1970–71 to over 66 per cent in 1991. (It can be hoped that by 2005 it has increased further and crossed 70 per cent). This is quite appreciable. However, it has also been noted that, at margin, farmers in India have to depend on the usurious money lender for finance. Thus the dream of the complete elimination of the money lender has not been realized even by the close of the 20th century.

It has also been observed that over the years, due to the falling demand for food grains (from the consumers) financing food grain production is gradually becoming difficult unlike under green revolution when there was assured demand from consumers as well as from the government. Also, due to the diversification of agriculture especially in the area of fruits and vegetables, there is growing need of finance. This, however, becomes difficult for the credit agencies due to the generally unsatisfactory marketing especially for the small farmers. The problem will have to be addressed.

As regards the fulfillment of the targeted amount of credit bankers appear to be sceptical about its achievement. It has been pointed out that since the growth of agricultural credit in the last decade of 20th Century has not been more than 16 per cent every year[10], an annual increase of 30 per cent in the amount of finance would be extremely difficult. Section IV below discusses the State of Indian agriculture.

INDIAN AGRICULTURE TODAY

In this section, we note some main points about Indian Agriculture, at present, without going deep in the analysis.

(a) Agriculture contributes around 20 per cent to the GDP. But employs, Directly & indirectly 70 per cent of labour.

(b) The fall in the contribution of agriculture to the GDP has been much faster than the fall in the percentage of labour dependent on agriculture.

(c) The disparity in the per capita income between agricultural and non agri. Sector has been rising. It was 1 to 2.19 (1950–51) and 1 to 4.35 (1989–90). It is likely to be more today.

(d) Per capita arable land has fallen due to pressure of population and also due to soil degradation. It was 0.37 ha. in 1950–51. It was 0.22 ha. in 1991[12]. percentage of small forms rising.

(e) Rate of growth has been highly uneven but disappointing on the whole. It was: –2.8 per cent (1997), 6.9 per cent (1998), –0.1 per cent (1999), –0.6 per cent (2000) & 5.7% (2001).

(f) Food availability per capita for Indian population has fallen from 510 gms/day/person (1991) to 438 gms/day/person in 2003[13]. Food security is available to many due to the wide spread poverty in the country.

(g) Diversification of agricultural production is considerably less even at present when around 70 per cent of land is still under food grains especially by small farmers.

(h) Poverty is concentrated in landless farm workers and the small farmers. Most of the employment for these classes in under employment. And

(i) Public capital formation in agriculture, has been falling but private capital formation is not rising sufficiently. Public capital formation was Rs. 4849 crores (1995–96). It fell to Rs. 4538 crores (2002–03)[14].

Clearly despite the strong efforts from the side of credit and finance, Indian agriculture, as a whole, appears to be underdeveloped and traditional. Section V below considers why it is so.

CREDIT AND AGRARIAN TRANSFORMATION

In this section, we discuss, as to why, inspite of all round efforts to provide credit to the farmers and inspite of some success in this matter, Indian agriculture as a whole has still not achieved the desirable degree of development and modernization, and transformation. The challenge here (to the credit provision) has been to convert the "nonviable" farmer into a "viable" one.

Out of all sources of the institutional credit to farming the "Co-operative credit" was regarded as the ideal and most desirable for India's agricultural development. Co-operative credit ably supported by the State was regarded as almost the panacea for agricultural development. However, inspite of the liberal assistance and support given by the RBI, the weaknesses and the non-viability of co-operative credit structure was recognized and by 1966 it was admitted that the co-operative credit sector would not be able to meet the demand for credit and an active role for the (nationalized) commercial banks was recommended. Thus, the predominant role of the Coop. Credit structure ended, by 1968–69.

However, even with the nationalized commercial banks the experience was not all that good. The problem of non recovery of loans, mounting over dues, almost a constant demand for refinance from the higher financial agencies like RBI and NABARD did not subside sufficiently. It was recognized that such things can threaten the financial health of the banking sector itself. The question "whether the targets of credit for the weaker and poor sections were unreasonably higher" began to be considered.

In this context "KHUSRO COMMITTEE" makes three highly pertinent observation: (a) The targets of credit for the weaker sections should be Reasonable such as the system can bear and more importantly (b) The weaknesses of institutional agricultural credit in India (Co-op, RRB and C.B.) are not inherent but they arise from the deficiencies of the structure of agricultural production itself, and (c) it is essential to recognize the limitations of credit as the means of agrarian transformation.[15] Thus it is at least a tacit admission by a high power committee that credit has failed to transform the small farmer dominated agrarian sector because the small cultivator is not "Potentially Viable". Let it not be forgotten that small farmers cultivate a substantial part of the total cultivable land but each in a small, Unviable, plot.

Thus in the attempt of developing the agricultural sector (i.e. small farmer) by means of credit for the last fifty years, all have lost viz, the farmer, the credit agencies and the agricultural sector. The remedy lies in making agriculture economically potentially viable and then supporting it with adequate credit. If this is not done the same experience about credit will repeat hereafter.

MAKING SMALL FARMER VIABLE

It is fact that agriculture as a whole is still not fully modernized inspite of new technology and provision of services like credit etc., for the last several years. It should therefore, be clear that the reason for the "non viability" of the small farmer is neither technology nor credit but it is the "Over crowding of agriculture"[16]. It appears that small farms would not became viable unless some population is with drawn from agriculture. But this is easily said than done. However, measures like freeing the land market, tenancy market and other measures consistent with the new economic policy of liberalization etc.[17] could be considered. Provision of credit alone can not do the job.

NOTES & REFERENCES

1. Jones, T.L. (1971), "Agricultural Credit Institutions" in Blace (ed.) Institutions in Agricultural Development", Iowa state University Press 1971.
2. Mellor , J.W. (1969), "The Economics of Agricultural Development Vora and Co. Bombay, p. 310.
3. Schultz, T.W. (1953), "Economic Organization of Agriculture McGraw Hill, p. 195.
4. Jones T.L. op cit,
5. Venkitramanam, S. (2004), "Case for Mitigating Lending Risks in" Business Line 20-12-2004.
6. Ibid.
7. Business Line 07-09-2004.
8. Venkit Ramanan op cit.
9. Ibid.
10. Business Line 02-03-2005.
11. Dandekar, V.M. (1993), "Limits of Credit: Not Credit Limits" in EPW 25-09-1993.
12. Business Line 06-08-2004.

13. The Economic Times. 28-07-2004.
14. Ibid.
15. Dandekar, op cit.
16. Dandekar, op cit.
17. Dendekar, op cit.

6

DISCUSSANT'S REPORT REFORMS IN IRRIGATION AND CREDIT SECTORS

D.M. More

Following two papers were presented during the Conference.

1. Irrigation Reforms in Maharashtra By Dr.S.G. Bhogale
2. Agricultural Development—limitations of credit by Dr. A.R. Padoshi

THE OBSERVATION MADE IN THE PAPERS ARE BRIEFLY NOTED DOWN BELOW

Reforms in Irrigation

During the last few years, Govt. of Maharashtra has been concentrating on bringing reforms in various sectors. Irrigation is one of the sectors. This is being done to improve the performance of the system. In other words there should be a discipline in the management of water, in fixing tariff, in recovering the water charges and so on. The operation and maintenance of the system will be with WUAs. The focus is to make the system sustainable.

- Policy reforms
- Administrative reforms
- Social reforms

Policy Reforms

Maharashtra Management of Irrigation System by Farmers Main features:

1. Water will be supplied only to WUAs
2. Supply on volumetric basis.
3. Freedom for cropping pattern.
4. Assured Assured supply to tail enders.
5. Distribution of water to farmers, be looked after by association.

State Water Policy

It is a vision document: It is there to provide greatest economic and social benefits to the people of the state.

State Water Regulatory Authority

1. It will regulate
   - (i) Sectoral allocation
   - (ii) Water rates
   - (iii) Changes in water use
   - (iv) Compensation for such changes.
2. Administrative reforms
   - (i) Water auditing
   - (ii) Water pricing
   - (iii) Bench marking
   - (iv) Application of modern irrigation methods
   - (v) Application of remote sensing
   - (vi) I.T.
3. Capacity building by imparting training.

Reforms in Credit

Credit as a means, for agricultural development.

1. Credit is essential for production, consumption and repayment purposes.

2. The percentage of small farmers is over -75%
3. Most of them are resource poor.
4. The agricultural credit in India is wholly Govt. initiated and Government sponsored.

Annual targets are fixed and the credit facilities are defused over a large no. of farmers. As today it has crossed 70%. At places farmers are dependent on the money lenders for finance.

Around 70% of command is still under food grains. Poverty is concentrated in land-less workers and small farmers. This class has not been adequately employed.

COMMENTS

Irrigation Reforms

What for reforms are made? What do we achieve by doing changes in the existing system?

As far as irrigation sector is concerned it is mainly for

1. Increasing the agricultural productivity.
2. Establishing social and economic equity.

The aim is to eradicate the inequality, disparity that exist in the society. The reforms are made not for creating pockets of prosperity. They are directed towards the overall economic growth of the masses.

Can an act/rule alone, introduce a change? The answer will be no. We have two classic events with us. (1) Anti Dowri Act and (2) Anti Copying Movement. Rules/acts have been made. Efforts were made to educate the people through different forums. Despite this, there has not been a change in this regard. On the contrary there has been increase in the incidents in these two areas. What could be the reason? The administration or the government wanted to establish discipline in these areas by eradicating the social evils. People at large did not consider that as necessary, for the sake of their own vested interest. In other words people's initiative was meagre. As a result inspite of all the laws and rules in vogue society did not change. It lacked people's participation and the legal changes made remained on paper, as ineffective.

On the background of this can we say that legal framework/ back up is not necessary. It is not so. For introducing a change in the society a legal weapon is utmost necessary, but that alone cannot be effective.

People must have trust in the administration. In the historical period in the early part of the 20th century, the King Chatrapati Shahu Maharaj introduced equity/judicious distribution of water, in irrigation through people's participation. He inspired people. He acted as a facilitator. People came forward, constructed weirs across river Panchaganga, lifted water through series of animal driven devices and brought large areas under irrigation through community efforts. This is a unique example. People had love for the King. They relied on and followed whatever the King said. There was no Act. People did on their own and acquired the height of prosperity through water. The support of the Administration was firm, come what may.

During 2002 or so, on one of the irrigation projects in Maharashtra the designated quota of water was not supplied to the group of societies located at tail end. As per the agreement between the society and government water was required to be given to the society on priority. The water was diverted/reserved for urban centres. What to do? The members of the association made an appeal for the release of required quota. They were moving from pillar to post. It was again politics. Who is in power? The association was advised to go to court for justice and so on. The layman's reaction was, it happens in democracy. What is democracy? People should behave, the way they like to behave. Is it not a law abiding society? The trust gets lost. This is a permanent loss.

There is another example i.e. of Latur City. It is a medium size town, population around 4 lac, historically famous, political capital for the liberation of Mahrathwada from the rules of Nijam of Hyderabad. In the historical period the city survived on ground water. It is situated on the bank of river Manjra. As usual during the course of time water supply was made available by the local administration and the traditional devices in the form of open wells, aads were made redundant. The entire population was made to rely on government run water supply scheme. The source has been the river Manjara and the Manjara reservoir at Dhanegaon. For last four years the reservoir is dry. The city water supply has gone to zero. This year (2004–05) the situation is also same. The shortage of water continues.

There is no unrest amongst the Society. There are no rallies, no columns in the newspapers. Very little could be done by the Government. People devised their own ways for quenching their thrust. It is a politically volatile place. Despite this the situation has been normal. What could be the reason? The administration has not made any law or rule nor any special efforts for maintaining law and order for making people quiet. People on their own realized the difficulties, they searched for the alternatives and got engaged in their routine activities as usual as if nothing has happened. Today one can see the roof water harvesting in every house for recharging the bore-water.

There is a Manar project. Its service area is around 25000 ha. It was commissioned sometime in late seventies. Till 2000, or so it was known as sugarcane project. There were sugar factories around and the sugarcane was marketed in the sugar factories. There after the picture is changed. Now there is no sugarcane. People have gone for crops like Soyabean, Groundnut, Sunflower, and Wheat. Once upon a time the entire water was consumed for growing sugarcane. Efforts were made then to change the cropping pattern. People did not change. Now without any efforts everybody has gone for other than sugarcane. The reason is non-functioning of sugar factories. There is no market for sugarcane. People have gone for marketable crops. The cropping pattern could be changed. The market governs the types of crops. The entire area is under irrigation. This is equity. The yield/income per drop is increased.

Since 1992 the Department of Irrigation has been striving hard to form water users Associations and hand over the irrigation management to them. The present picture is, there are about 800 societies on 2 lac ha. The average rate is less than 20, 000 ha. per year. This shows that there is a slow growth. Now we have made an Act. We expect this will be done at a faster rate. The regionwise analysis shows that in Konkan and Vidharbha a beginning is yet to be made. There is no water users society in Kolhapur area.

The above events (dowry, Latur, Manar etc.) teach a lot. There has to be an attitudinal change in the society, then only the Act becomes effective. We have to strive hard in this direction.

There are issues, which need attention. We have (1) measuring devices (2) diversion of water for urban centres (3) norms for domestic consumption (4) recycling of water (5) area under lift irrigation (6) overlapping command (7) individual lifts (8) fixing of water tariff and so on. We need to study the Andhra Pradesh model. There, it is learnt, Act was made and overnight the Irrigation projects were handed over to the Water User's Associations for irrigation management purpose. The project was funded by World Bank. During the initial period the Societies were given financial aid/grant for rectification of the distribution system. The aid might have been stopped by now. People have to take over on their own and maintain the system here in after. Let us hope that the system is under proper functioning.

It is an era of information technology. You generate information, tabulate systematically. The tables give some results. You bank on those arrived conclusions. Science/Mathematics cannot be wrong, so the tables. Projecting the future on the basis of conclusions drawn from the tables might lead to an area of un-fulfillment. We have to be careful. The inference may not lead to reality.

CREDIT SECTOR

Indian agricultural as a whole appears to be under developed and traditional. The literate class migrates to urban centres. The farming is thus dependent on the young illiterates and the old ones. Those who do not work they have a status, *thus there is no dignity to labour.*

The land is fragmented. The per capita availability of land is around 0.2 hectors. This is further decreasing. Thus the farming has become unviable.

Why Unviable?

1. Prices-erratic.
2. Fragmentation of land.

3. Potentially unviable
4. No water for protective irrigation
5. No soft loan/credit.

The credit has failed to transform the *small farmer dominated agricultural sector as it is not potentially viable.* The small farmer cultivates around 50% of the total cultivable land, but each on a small unviable plot. The remedy lies in making agriculture potentially viable & then supporting it with adequate credit. The vast tract under dry farming needs to be treated *immediately through soil and water conservation techniques and dry land farming be* transformed into double cropping area. The over *crowding of agriculture is another issue.* Efforts need to be made to divert a big chunk of labour force elsewhere. *Agro industry could be an alternative area.*

The subsidy benefits go to elite people, industrialists and not to the poor. The credit facility should be at cheaper rates. It should be a soft loan. There have been cases where the bank's interest had gone beyond 50%. These interest rates are inclusive of penal-rate, service charges, everything compounded together & so on. The farmers are required to sell their piece of land for repayment. Such cases are large in number.

The main Agenda for eradicating poverty of rural area/Agri. sector, should be, see that water is made available to a large portion of cultivable land.

1. By way of surface storages.
2. By way of improving ground water.

This has to be done in a definite time frame.

7

STATE LEVEL ECONOMIC REFORMS: WITH SPECIAL REFERENCE TO INFRASTRUCTURE SECTOR OF KARNATAKA

M.G. Basava Raja, T. Ramesh
Manu Mahesh & M.D. Umesh

The progress of economic reforms in India during the last 13 years has been reasonably good but further reforms need to be put in place to ensure higher economic growth rate. Government of India is continuing with the reforms package for industrial sector so as to ensure that the Indian economy achieves the eight per cent growth rate in the country in the coming year. For this, large scale customs and excise rationsation personal tax reforms, restructuring of the banking sector, policies facilitating greater flow of foreign direct investment, infrastructural development, fastening of reforms at the State level, improvement in the financial health of the states etc., need to give high priority. Industries are geographically situated in the states, and are subject to rules and regulations applied by the states in authorizing the installation of plants and in ensuring that they operate within the framework of existing laws and rules, whereas Union Government has been busy in dismantling controls and changing rules in its own domain, states are advised by the Union Government to speed up reforms at various levels to set right their dismal state of financial health. This paper intends to concentrate on State Level Economic Reforms with special reference to infrastructure development in the States along with Karnataka Experience.

FINANCIAL HEALTH OF THE STATES

Financial health of many states is not good. As indicated in the Economic Survey Reports, the Report of the Twelfth Finance Commission, Union Budget for 2005–06, the revenue account of States has been in deficit since 1987–88.

The deterioration of financial conditions of States has been more pronounced from the late 1990s. According to N.J. Kurien Study Group Report of Planning Commission (1990–91 to 1998–99) the dismal state of financial health of states is largely owing to the poor financial Performance of State Public Sector Undertaking (PSUs) which need to go a long way to ensure a modicum of reforms on the huge capital sunk.

As much as 90% of the accumulated losses was incurred by Andhra Pradesh, Assam, Delhi, Gujrath, Karnataka, Kerala, Maharashtra, Orissa, Punjab, Tamil Nadu, Uttar Pradesh and West Bengal. Delhi and West Bengal are the loss leaders, with Assam, Uttar Pradesh, Kerala and Tamil Nadu following. The manufacturing and utility categories of state PSUs incurred losses consistently with utility enterprises from power and transport emerging as the principal loss markers.

AN OVERVIEW OF STATE LEVEL ECONOMIC REFORMS IN INDIA

In the context of studying state level economic reforms, the study of relationship between fiscal reforms and PSU reforms is of same importance. Budgets of the states are paying a heavy price for the maintenance of their PSUs at the present state of their dismal financial condition. The PSUs are maintained as at present by imposing higher taxes or by resorting to the exorbitant borrowings. The major portion of the loans and investments by the states are made to the PSUs. Because of their losses, they do not repay the loans or pay the interest or declare a dividend. In addition to extending loans directly, the states had been guaranteeing the loans to PSUs by the financial institutions. Often, these guarantees are invoted and the states are forced to pay aggravating the budgetary crisis. The need of the hour appears to be to fastern State Level Economic Reforms.

The economic reforms introduced by the Union Government have made sufficient provision for the states to introduce economic reforms at the state level and attract private capital in the fields of power, irrigation, road, parks, and all areas of industry. As rightly stated in World Bank Study Report headed by Zoubida Allaon, it is the ability of the state to attract private capital which determines a states' growth performance. The flows of private capital to a particular state, among others, is depending upon investor-friendly environment (IFE). The IFE encompasses an advanced infrastructure, skilled working class, investor friendly rules and regulations and moderate tax policy. Significant reforms are needed to bring this about in the states of India.

PRE-REQUISITES FOR STATE LEVEL REFORMS

(i) Policy pricing, institutional and regulatory reforms to induce private sector to invest in infrastructure into commercially viable projects and improvements in the capacity of states to manage commercially enforceable contracts;

(ii) An environment suitable to efficient public investment in areas where the public sector will remain important such as roads and urban services;

(iii) Public expenditure reforms to set aside unnecessary spending, and make room for priority programmes in public infrastructure, health and education; and

(iv) Tax reforms to provide stable sources of revenue at a low efficiency cost.

According to World Bank Report, policy, pricing and institutional reforms of key sectors would bring about the needed fiscal restructuring in the States power and irrigation reforms would help to increase fiscal gains in virtually all the states of the country. In states like Maharashtra, Karnataka, Gujrath, policy, pricing and institutional reforms alone, would be sufficient to restore fiscal sustainability. In other states, like Andhra Pradesh, Rajastan, Tamil Nadu, West Bengal, Haryana, putting the states public finances on a substainable path would require more comprehensive reforms of public expenditures such as public enterprise reforms, freeze on public employment, reduction in consumption subsidies; and for some of the states, a rationalization and retargeting of welfare programmes. In backward states such as Orissa, Bihar and Uttar Pradesh, sectoral reforms and public expenditure restructuring may need to be complemented by debt refinancing.

INFRASTRUCTURE POLICY REFORMS AT THE STATE LEVEL

In India, PSUs of Union Government and States have traditionally been responsible for the development of infrastructure facilities. Considerable resources have been invested in telecommunications, power and transport with mixed results. While the industrial sector has been growing rapidly, additions and improvements to infrastructure have been not adequate to keep up with demand. The demand for basic infrastructure has also been followed by the increasing number of foreign investors setting up factories in the country to produce manufactured goods. Infrastructure constraints have also been compounded by poor management and the inefficient pricing of resources.

Most of PSUs involved in infrastructure development do not posses the adequate managerial ability nor economic strength needed to oversee the much-needed expansion of infrastructure. The issue of inadequate infrastructure facilities must be resolved if the country is to achieve the targeted growth rate of eight per cent. Government of India and various states have opened up their public utility industries to private sector both domestic and foreign. In the telecommunications industry, the Union Government not only allowed foreign companies to build and operate the telecommunications network, the companies may even be given the option of renewing their licenses after 15 years, effectively owing the networks in the networks in the interim.

The need to overcome the infrastructural bottlenecks is becoming a critical issue for all the states. In the changed global scenario, any delay in the planned infrastructure projects make the states less competitive and might even stunt their economic growth. Regarding commercialization of infrastructural facilities, the progress in the states is not adequate. Hence, Government of India has directed the states to speed up infrastructure reform policies. Several states have already started the implementation of reforms in the infrastructure sector particularly in the fields of power, parks, roads and restructuring of public expenditure and in the revenue front.

POWER SECTOR REFORMS

Power sector used to run by State Electricity Board (SEBs). They were responsible for generating and distributing power, setting tariffs and collecting revenue. Due to power theft, social subsidy scheme, transmission losses, accumulation heavy amount of dues and interest, SEBs of majority of states were incurring losses.

In power sector, recognising the fact that SEBs credit worthiness must be restored to attract private capital, Karnataka, Maharashtra, Tamil Nadu, Andhra Pradesh and other states have introduced power sector reforms which endorse (i) establishment of an independent regulatory agency (ii) tariffs reflecting costs (iii) competition among independent power producers (iv) divestiture of shares in the power generating PSUs and restructuring and privatization of the distribution functions of the SEBs. This approach has laid out in a Common Minimum National Action Plan for Power (CMAP 1996) issued by Union Ministry of Power, on the basis of agreements reached in Chief Ministers Conferences. Steps have been taken to implement tariff reforms in various states which include the following:

1. Higher prices actually collected on electricity use is the first order of business.
2. Privatization of power generation and the conversion of SEBs from power providers to market regulators would come next.

3. Power capacity will not be expanded until the SEBs are fundamentally overhauled or eliminated.
4. Even private power projects were expected to sell their electricity to the SEBs as they were the power purchasers; so that the bank ability of private sector power projects depended fundamentally on the financial health of the SEBs.

WATER SUPPLY REFORMS

In water, investment for rehabilitation and modernization (RM) along with volume-based pricing and institutional changes would provide the basis for efficient water use, cost recovery and improved service delivery in canal irrigation. The RM of irrigation schemes would restore the reliability of water delivery without which farmers will be reluctant to pay higher water charges.

The RM Irrigation scheme makes provision for the introduction of volume-based pricing of water management practices. Institutional reforms like formation of Water Users' Associations, provide the basis and necessary financial incentives for improved cost recovery as well as improved accountability in the delivery of water services to farmers. Tamil Nadu, Andhra Pradesh and Orissa have started (1997) reforms with the objectives of the cost recovery, quality of service delivery to farmers, and systems turn over to water users. In its 1995 agricultural policy Karnataka state proposed radically to transform institutional incentives in the irrigation sector. Even through there is wider scope for private participation in urban water supply some reform-minded municipalities have been nonetheless successful in attracting private capital and expertise.

PWD REFORM

Reforming the Public Works Departments removes main obstacle to efficient road construction. To overcome the capacity constraints of PWDs, private professional engineering firms have to be contracted to investigate and design large costly sections of road suitable for construction by machine intensive methods alone. The World Bank Team has suggested for downsizing and retraining of in-house PWD engineering staff. This means a smaller but very important role for State PWDs as planner, administrator and maintainer of roads. The professional engineering firms investigates and design roads, supervise construction and maintenance and supply material and equipment. The PWD reforms are implemented in various states and roads are being constructed on international standards.

REFORMS OF PORTS

Ports of India face capacity shortage and low productivity levels. Government of India has implemented several measures for improving the institutional framework and induce private investment to ports. Maritime States have implemented similar reforms to develop their ports and relieve major ports. Some states have identified projects worth $ one billion to develop their medium ports. However, according to World Bank Team, despite the attractiveness of such investments to the private sector, they are considered a complement to, but not a full substitute for, investments by the states or individual port trusts.

URBAN REFORMS

Town and Cities (TCs) are facing under investment and shortages of key services. The problems of TCs relate to the weak fiscal base-eroded by state law imposing rent controls, limits on the amount of land an individual can hold, restrictions on land markets, and unrealistically low water rates. In some of TCs, revenues are excessively dependent on inefficient taxes which need to be eliminated. According to the World Bank, the Urban Reforms need the following measures.

(a) Improving the use of the existing resource base like better cost recovery and enforcement of existing taxes.

(b) Strengthening of the resource base and make it more efficient which include lifting of rent controls in the major cities, eliminating octroi, setting up of efficient land markets with an effective system of land titling and

(c) Need for establishing a rule-based, efficient system of capital grants to replace the present system.

These measures help to provide the basis for the restoration of the finances of the urban areas and thus restore their capacity to invest in critically needed infrastructure. These measures would also help urban governments become credit worthy borrowers, able to access capital markets and raise funds for critically needed investments. Already, various states have introduced some of these measures, by providing access to capital markets and in turn these measures have provided incentives for urban governments to improve their financial management.

REFORMING OF PUBLIC EXPENDITURE OF THE STATES

One of the important challenges of the states is to improve cost recovery by eliminating explicit and implicit subsidies, and reduce unproductive expenditures. In various states, some progress has been made in restructuring public expenditure with a view to reducing unproductive expenditure. For example, there is growing recognition of the need to control recruitment to reduce the wage bill, eliminate poorly targeted welfare programmes, and privatize PSUs. In order to limit the interest burden, a more careful selection of projects based on their rate of return needs to be established. PSUs need to be subjected to hard budget constraint by discontinuing the practice of converting debt to equity. Privatisation of PSUs engaged in activities that could be provided more efficiently by the private sector, could provide considerable efficiency and fiscal gains.

REVENUE REFORMS

Revenue reforms are needed to increases cost recovery as an essential part of sectoral reforms, broaden the base, improve the efficiency of taxation, and ensure tax harmonization across states. Major states need to take the lead in ensuring that states collectively adhere to recommendations to State Finance Ministers' committee (Dec 1995) to do away with incentives and concessions for industrial investments and harmonise their sales tax policies. The acceleration of state's sales tax reforms could help the establishment of a VAT.

REFORMING OF THE DESIGN OF INTER GOVERNMENTAL TRANSFERS

Efforts are needed to ensure that the funds borrowed by the states from the Central Government (and also from other sources) are used only for such investment expenditures that yield a return adequate to meet the cost of borrowing, which should reflect a states credit worthiness. The latter would provide strong incentives to improve their fiscal management.

The above narrated World Bank suggestions help the states to raise funds for making investment in rural infrastructure and human resources thus arresting recent declines. State subsidies account for seven per cent of GDP, this works out to almost twice of India's total spending on health and education. Spending on health and education are not only a small share of total state GDP but this share has been declining. There is room to enhance efficiency of service deliver, cost effectiveness, and allocation of expenditure. But spending needs to increase as well. To achieve universal enrollment and higher quality education states have to increase their real outlays for primary education. The same type of dilemma confronts the states with the lowest levels of health care, where per capita Government spending is low to meet the promise of insuring universal access to care in Primary Health Centres (PHCs). Increasing public expenditures for health by roughly half needs to be kept as a goal, but in the fiscally straightend circumstances of many states, it may be more realistic in the short term to aim for a phased reorientation of outlays so that ¾ th of them go to the primary and secondary sectors with priority given to the provision of medicines and essential supplies.

ECONOMIC REFORMS-KARNATAKA EXPERIENCE

Karnataka one of the country's fastest growing states, and an icon of liberalization, exhibits some typical characteristics of a reforming economy. It was the only state to have experienced a growth rate of eight per cent in the second half of 1990s. It has undertaken a series of economic reforms which have been supported by a World Bank Assistance package (Rs. 12000 crore) to cover six major projects. These include restructuring plan of Rs. 5000 crore for a period of four years (2002–06). This plan covers power sector reforms, public expenditure reforms, transition to VAT and governance reforms. Others in the aid package are the state high ways, water shed management, rural water supply and management and desiltation of tanks.

INDUSTRY AND INFRASTRUCTURE REFORMS

Karnataka has undertaken several procedural and policy reforms for industrial development, promoting foreign investment, encouraging private sector in the development of infrastructure and the development and management of industrial estates/ industrial areas, restructuring of industry promoting institutions etc.

The thrust of the industrial policy reform of Karnataka is on building up of infrastructure in areas such as power generation, express high ways, industrial parks, townships, Air ports and ports with active participation of private sector. The industrial reforms of the state intends to replace the 'Bureaucratic Approach' with an advanced 'Professional Outlook'. More specifically, industrial reforms can be enumenated as given below:

1. Simplification of rules and regulations concerning the establishment of industrial units.
2. Making provision for the private participation in the field of infrastructure development.
3. Permission for the conversion of land into non-agricultural use.
4. Policy on spatial diversification in industrial development.
5. Expediting the decision making process for the non-resident Indians and Foreign direct investment (NRI and FDI)
6. Opening up of Single Window Agency for speedy clearing of industrial and infrastructural projects.
7. Tax concessions for certain industries.
8. Measures of providing of better quality of services, power, infrastructural facilities and improvement in the quality of higher education and training.

9. Liberalization of inter-state barriers, check posts, collection points on national highways or what ever.
10. Tax Reforms.

Karnataka has designated nodal agencies under the Directorate of Industries and Commerce to promote industrial investment in the State.

Karnataka Udyog Mitra acts as the single window clearing agency and offers escort services for proposals under Rs. 50 Crore, the Karnataka Industrial Areas Development Board acquires land, develops, and allots to the entrepreneurs for establishing industrial units.

To tide over the major problem of inadequate infrastructure—power, water road—the Government is wooing investors in these high priority areas and a Mega Infrastructure programme is launched in the state. The joint venture Bangalore International Air Port Project at Devanahally, the private promoted Bangalore-Mysore Toll Express Way and Infrastructure Corridor; upgradation of the minor Air ports; development of minor Sea ports, and a World Bank funded upgradation of state highways are all part of this mega agenda.

Active as a show piece of all these impressive achievements is Bangalore, which earned a firm foot hold in the world technology map through its hugely successful strides in software development. For the record, the technology—driven city is adjudged as one of the ten hottest tech cities of the world by famous international business periodicals—News Week and Business Week.

POWER SECTOR REFORMS

In August 1999, the Karnataka Electricity Reforms Bill was enacted. The Karnatka Electricity Board is corporatised into the Karnataka Power Transmission Corporation Ltd. (KPTCL) and more importantly the Karnataka Electricity Regulatory Commission is established. The State Government has invited private sector participation in the distribution of electricity in the state. Government intends to attempt privatisation of all companies simultaneously and complete the process in a period of two years.

The State Government has unbundled the distribution function of KPTCL and four undependent state owned electricity supply compances (ESCOMS) have been formed on regional basis viz., Bangalore Electricity Supply Company (BESCOM), Hubli Electricity Supply Company (HESCOM), Mangalore Electricity Supply Company (MESCOM) and Gulbarga Electricity Supply Company (GESCOM). These companies are assigned distribution and retail supply licnese of KPTCL after getting approval from KERC. In tune with the state policy, these companies are taking several reforms to improve the quality of power supply to consumers, establish proper system of energy accounting, metering and recovery.

Table 1
Generation, Imports, T and D Losses and Consumption of Power in Karnataka

Year	*Power Generation installed capacity (MSW)*	*Electricity Generation (million units)*	*Imports (million units)*	*T and D losses (%)*	*Power Consumption (million units)*
1999–2000	4423.87	21092	6056	38.00	16151
2000–2001	4525.14	21119	6621	35.50	17867
2001–2002	4411.54	19214	7609	35.86	18639
2002–2003	4699.03	18105	9043	30.70	19888
2003–2004	4714.03	17625	10000	NA	20500

Source: Government of Karnataka (2004) Economic Survey 2003–04. (Bangalore: Planning and Statistics Department).

The state Government has announced implementation of three year metering programme to complete metering all unmetred consumers and to set up full scale energy audit. Accordingly, a policy direction has issued to change the IP set consumers as per actual energy consumed or at HP rates which ever is lower. This measure is intended to increase the acceptability and accelerate universal metering programme. All the ESCOMS are taking steps to implement this programme.

The state has come out with its revised independent power producers policy with a clearly delineated "no Escrow" stance. Escrow cover relates to the financial security package an IPP demands from the Government for producing power.

Over 16 lakhs beneficiaries under the Bhagyajyothi and Kuteera Jyothi schemes would be given only 18 units of free electricity per month henceforth. The state has also decided to waive off Rs. 157 crore arrears from these beneficiaries following unrestricted power supply. It is also decided in the state to regularize 1.35 lakh un-authorised pumsets owned by people and allow them to install metres by paying yearly minimum deposit of Rs. 10000 and Rs. 2000 towards installment charges.

TRANSPORT REFORMS

Road Reforms

Karnataka has launched massive road construction programme. One of the major initiatives is the World Bank assisted High Ways Improvement Project, which covers, 2,263 kms of roads. In this high ways sector, five major schemes have been sanctioned and they are:

1. Golden quadrilateral scheme covering 625 kms at a cost of Rs. 320 crores.
2. The new National Highway NH 218 announced by the Union Government.
3. North-South and East-West Corridor connecting Kashmir and Kanyakumari and Silchar to Saurashtra respectively.
4. The Central Road Fund Scheme, which is only extended to national high ways covers state high ways and major district roads.
5. Cable-stayed bridge over the railway line of Krishnarajapuram at a cost of Rs. 42 crore.

In the state high ways sector, the state Government has taken major initiatives (i) The establishment of the Karnataka Road Development Corporation Ltd., (KRDCL) to moblise resource from financial institutions (ii) the decision of entrusting road maintenance to private agencies.

Apart from Central and State high ways, the State Government has also launched massive programme to improve roads in the districts under major districts road programme (MDRP). Karnataka has witnessed major strides in building and maintenance of bridges with HUDCO assistance. The State Government has launched four major projects for improving the Bangalore-Mysore, Mysore-Bantwal, Belur-Belikere and Jewargi-Bijapur ring roads. Work on the State High Ways Maintenance Project is progressing in respect of 7000 km, private sector participation is envisaged for a period of three years in the HUDCO assistance.

Table 2
Road Length in Karnataka (in Kms)

Year	*National Highways*	*State Highways*	*Major District Roads*	*All Roads**
1991–1992	1997	11288	18063	133987
1992–1993	1997	11288	28169	134592
1993–1994	1997	11395	28139	134832
1994–1995	1997	11395	28284	135104
1995–1996	1997	11395	2831	137520
1996–1997	1997	11395	28311	137520
1997–1998	2355	11037	28361	142801
1998–1999	3524	10021	28247	144846
1999–2000	3728	9829	28247	148589
2000–2001	3728	9829	28247	154204
2002–2002	3728	9829	28247	154204

* National + State Highways, Major District Roads, others District Roads Municipal Roads, other Roads.

Source: Government of Karnataka (2004) Economic Survey 2003–04. (Bangalore: Planning and Statistics Department).

The State Government has almost completed a massive scheme of construction of 19 flyovers in Bangalore. Another initiative of Karnataka is the Bangalore-Mysore Infrastructure corridor project taken up by NICEL on BOOT basis (Rs. 2000 crores project). This involves construction of an express high way of 111 Kms, Peripheral Roads of over 41 km, Link roads of 9.10 km and elevated roads of 3 kms and development of five Townships. The BMIC will help to reduce the travel time between Bangalore and Mysore from three hours to one hour and 15 minutes.

The Panchayat Raj and Rural Development Department is developing rural roads by investing Rs. 92 crores under the PMs

Sadak Yojana. With these major on going projects and other ambitions proposals, the public works department is poised for a radical transformation.

METRO RAIL PROJECT

MRP has been conceived as a joint venture of the State Government and the Union Government along with debt raised from nearly 20 FIs led by UTI Bank. For MRP while state Government will provide Rs. 1807 crores, the Union Government would contribute Rs. 1447 crores and the FIs the remaining Rs. 2953 crores. The first train from Bangalore is expected to run by October 2008.

Bangalore Mass Rapid Transit Ltd. (BMRTL) has been entrusted with the task of planning, designing and land acquisition, any shifting of utilities in the way and short listing of contractors and vendors for the MRP. The land for MRP would include 102 acres from the defence authorities, 55 acres from the State Government and 40 acres from private owners. A 7-KM stretch would be built underground around Vidhana Soudha and the rest would be elevated.

URBAN WATER SUPPLY REFORMS

For this scheme, the World Bank has extended financial assistance of Rs. 237.07 crores. Karnataka Urban Infrastructure and Finance Corporation is the nodal agency for this scheme. Under this scheme 24 hours water will be supplied in Municipal Corporation Areas of Belgaum, Gulbarga, Hubli-Dharwad. This is a novel scheme of checking the leakage in the water supply and utilizing locally available water sources. If this scheme is succeeded it will be extended other Urban Centres of the State.

SANITATION REFORMS

To make cities lovable and livable, there is need for proper management of city wastes. In Karnataka, the waste management project is taken up jointly with German Cooperation (GIZ) which is providing financial assistance to the tune of Euro 1.5 million. The solid wastes and effluent waters are being treated and bio-manure is produced by private entrepreneurs in cities like Bangalore, Mysore and other places.

PORTS REFORMS

The ports policy of Karnataka adopted a strategy to use private investment for the creation of port facilities, development of new sites and supporting infrastructure, maritime related industries and coastal shipping and port facilities for power projects. The Karnataka State Industrial Investment and Development Corporation has been appointed as nodal agency for the implementation of this policy. A committee has been constituted to finalize the framework agreement with private companies. Private participation is allowed for three ports namely Belekere, Tadri and Old Mangalore.

Government of India, has announced its decision to go in for joint ventures between major ports and foreign ports, between major and minor ports, and major ports and Indian companies for improvement of port infrastructure. Under this joint venture, a scheme has been formulated for construction of additional berths at Karwar port to meet the anticipated Cargo growth and sent to New Mangalore Port Trust.

IRRIGATION REFORMS

The cumulative irrigation potential under major, medium and minor irrigation increased to 30.91 lakh hectares in 2003–2004 from 29.35 lakhs hectares in 2002–2003. Additional potential of 1.56 lakhs hectares is created in 2003–2004.

Karnataka has announced state water policy in January 2002. The salient features of the policy can be enumerated as given below.

1. Providing drinking water at the rate of 55 litres per person per day in rural area, 70 litres per persons per day in towns and 100 litres per person per day in the city municipal council areas and 135 litres per person per day in city corporation areas.
2. Creation of an ultimate irrigation potential of 45 lakh hectares. Facilities creation of an additional irrigation potential of 16 lakhs hectares by individual farmers using ground water.
3. Improving performance of all water resources projects.
4. Improving productivity of irrigated agriculture by involving users in irrigation management.

5. Harnessing the hydro potential in the state.
6. Providing a legislative, administrative and infrastructrual environment, which will ensure fair, just and equitable distribution and utilization of the water resources of the state to benefit all the people of the state.

COMMUNITY BASED TANK MANAGEMENT PROJECT

Karnataka has sought the World Bank's permission to utilize saved funds to rejuvenate 700 more tanks under the Rs. 678 crore Community Based Tank Management Project. The State hopes to save upto Rs. 140 crores from the project, targeted to review 2005 tanks in nine districts by 2008–09. As many as 270 tanks has been rejuvenated till now.

The project has planned to cumulative target to complete the revival of over 600 tanks under the Jala Samvardhana Yojana Project by the end of June 2005. The project promoted the Madagascar method of Paddy cultivation among the beneficiaries for getting more yield with less water. The State Government has recovered 89 hectares of land encroached upon in tank areas and it is planning to bring in a law against encroachment of tanks.

ACTION POINTS FOR THE STATE GOVERNMENTS

The foregoing description is indicative of the action expected from the states in various crucial areas, the important among which can be enumerated as given below

Governance Reforms

Corruption and poor governance are the first and the foremost areas to be set right by the states. There should be proper training and motivation for the Ministers, peoples' representatives and the Bureancrats in the fields of administration, development aspects and values in life. Efficient, and honest administration help to go a long way in achieving economic development of the States. Government of India and the States are borrowing heavy amount of funds from the foreign sources and financial institutions by paying exorbitant rate of interest. This fund should be used in an economic and efficient manner for the building of income giving assets in the country. The states should see that borrowed funds should generate adequate income to facilitate for the repayment to the lenders. This will go a long way in reducing fiscal deficit and increasing growth rate of the states and the country as a whole.

Irrigation Sector Reforms

Irrigation sector is very vital for the development of rural areas of States. The incessant poverty is, among other largely due to lack of irrigation facilities to the farmers. Fund shortage should not come in the way of taking up of irrigation projects. Water resources available in the states should not go waste. These funds borrowed for the irrigation sector should be utilized carefully to complete the projects in the stipulated time to overcome the problem of cost escalation. Proper reforms need to be introduced to recover the cost of development of irrigation projects to facilitate repayment to the lenders. Irrigation projects should be followed by proper forestation, fishery development programmes to create additional sources of income and employment.

Power Sector Reforms

Power sector reforms are bit withered in the states due to competitive populism among political parties. In the name of poor, rich are getting the benefit in the field of power. Deeper probe in the matter is needed. Unfortunately, most political parties have drawn wrong message from the 2004 electron result and trying to put the persuit of reforms process on the backburner. This appears to be more so in the case of PSRs, going by the way the State Governments (Andhra Pradesh, Tamil Nadu, Mahrashtara to name a few) have been vying with one another in offering free power to farmers, throwing all caution and fiscal prudence to winds. Power may be supplied free of cost to too poor farmers but this must be followed by proper check of power theft by the rich people belonging to different sectors of the economy.

There are also other ill effects of free power to farm sector such as the farmers using obsolete power guzzling pumpsets, not bothering to switch off the pumpsets leading to enormous wastage of water and growing more water using crops like paddy and sugar cane. As a result, the water deposits has been going down at an alarming rate. If the States continues with the practice of supplying free power to any group of consumers, it will not inspire private investors to invest on a massive scale in a sick industry.

Unbundling measures of SEBs are of vital importance not only for inducing private investment but also to deal with the serious problems encountering the power sector such as gross mismanagement, rampant corruption and large scale power thefts. It is open secret that a considerable proportion of the so called transmission and distribution losses are in fact power theft. According to one estimate, India could save $ 12 billion merely by improving efficiency in power generation and removing transmission and distribution bottlenecks, as it will drastically reduce the new capacity requirement.

Infrastructure Reforms

Still there is wider scope for private participation in the development of infrastructural facilities. If it is not possible to reduce public sector investment in infrastructure development as pointed out by Rakesh Mohan, the corresponding implication should be that the public sector infrastructure investment will have to be commercially viable.

In many states, the progress of infrastructure reforms especially in the field of irrigation is not adequate. Definitely private investment in the field of development of irrigation facilities will help to utilize available water resources in an economic and efficient manner. This will go a long way in improving the economic conditions of the people of rural areas of the States.

One of the most important items in the list of hurdles to the country's economic growth is poor infrastructural facilities. This is especially true of the transport sector. If ports are to be de-congested, proper roads constructed and the large but rickety rail network brough on track, India must invest significantly and without undue delay. But with the fiscal deficit hovering at around 10% of GDP and committed expenditures difficult to cut, there is need to find alternative sources of fund. M.S. Ahluwalia, the Deputy Chairman of Planning Commission some time back suggested the idea of drawing the funds ($ 5 billion a year) from the foreign exchange reserves of the country. Precisely, Union Finance Minister P.Chidambaram's Budget for 2005–06, proposes a special purpose vehicle (SPV)to implement the infrastructure projects that are financially viable but encounter problems in mobilizing resources. The FM wants to draw on the foreign exchange reserves, especially for project imports. Also, there is need for releasing certain norms governing external commercial borrowings (ECBs) to enable Indian Companies borrow abroad at lower cost for making investment in the financially viable infrastructure projects.

Transport is emerged as the principal loss makers of the States along with power. As suggested by Planning Commission Study Group, the Road Transport Corporations need to improve bus-staff ratio, occupancy ratio, fleet management and estate management practices. The innovative involvement of the private sector in the fleet could also improve their earnings.

Fiscal Reforms

Government of India's efforts to improve and strengthen the finances of the States is a healthy development but the most important aspect is that the states themselves have to participate in the process of fiscal consolidation. The economic reforms of the States should aim at reducing unproductive public expenditures, improving the economic performance of PSUs and making infrastructural facilities commercially viable.

CONCLUDING REMARKS

The economic reforms introduced in the country in the mid—1991 have created new dynamism and their progress in the last 13 years has been reasonably good. The ER policy measures are percolated gradually, from centre where they were initiated to the States in a considerable way. In the past several years, various political parties belonging to different ideology have come to power in the States and the Centre. They have taken up and continue to sustain bold economic reform measures embracing a wide range of activities to set right their dismal financial health. The ERs implemented so far have helped India to attain on an average more than five per cent growth. This can be considered as a legitimate achievement of the economic reforms. Still there is long way to go. Government of India and the States need to fasten reforms at the State level to check prevalent rampant corruption, to improve the efficiency in administration and quality in development works.

The public expenditure policy should be reoriented in such a way as to reduce unproductive expenditures and increase public spending in high priority areas such as development of irrigation facilities and other social and economic infrastructural facilities. The ER measures should also aim at inducing private investment in eco-friendly economic activities such as small wind and hydropower generation, biomass, municipal solid waste management and production of bio-manure and sugar factory cogeneration projects, development of parks, Tourism centres, etc., when all these measures are undertaken in earnest, it is likely to attain and sustain targeted eight per cent of economic growth.

REFERENCES

Ahluwalia, Montek S. (2003), "The Economic Performance of the States in the Post Reforms Period" in Ed. Kapila, Uma., Indian Economy Since Independence (New Delhi, Academic Foundation).

Datta, Ruddar (2000), "Second Generation Reforms: Need for Changing Growth Strategy", IEA 83rd Conference Volume.

Editorial (2005), "Funding Infrastructure" The Hindu Business Line Vol. 12, No. 68, March 10.

George, K.K. (2002), "Major Issues in State Level Fiscal Reforms" IEA 85th Conference Volume.

Godbole, Madhav (2002), "Power Sector Reforms: If Wishes were Horses" EPW Vol. XXXVII, No.7, Feb.16.

Government of Karnataka (2002), "Karnataka—Tomorrow's Destination Today, Advertiser's Feature" The Hindu, January 10.

Government of Karnataka (2004), "Economic Survey 2003–04" (Bangalore: Planning and Statistics Department).

Gurumurthy, S. (2002), "Twelfth Finance Commission and States' Debt Burden" EPW Vol. XXXVII, No. 40, October 5.

Heggade, Odeyar D. and Bharath M.R. (2000), "Second Generation Economic Reforms in India: Issues and Directions", IEA 83rd Conference Volume.

Jayanth, V. (2005), "States and Their Finances" the Hindu March 7, 128, No. 55.

Kurien, N.J. (2005), "Report of the Study Group on State Finances, Planning Commission, Press Report. The Hindu, April 16.

Naik, S.D. (2004), "Power Sector Reforms May Derail" The Hindu Business Line Vol. 11, No. 222, August 10.

Palande, P.S. (2000), "Coping with Liberalisation—The Industry's Response to New Competition" (New Delhi : Response Books).

Prasad, K.N. (2003), "Indian Economy—Before and Since the Reforms" IV, (New Delhi, Atlantic Publishers and Distributors).

Rangarajan, C. (2004), "Restructuring Public Finances for Equitable Growth—Issues Before the Twelfth Finance Commission". EPW, Vol. XXXIX, No. 26, June 26.

Rao, S.L. (2003), "Electricity Bill, 2001, Many Shortcoming, But a Step Forward" EPW, XXXVIII, No. 5, Feb. 1–7.

Shankar, T.L. (2002) "Towards a People's Plan for Power Sector Reforms" EPW, Vol. XXXVII, No. 40, Oct. 5–11.

Singa, Sidharth (2005), "Introducing Competition in the Power Sector: Open Access and Cross Subsides" EPW, Vol. XL, No. 7, Feb. 12.

World Bank (1997), India: Sustaining Rapid Economic Growth, A World Bank Country Study (Washington DC: The World Bank).

8

IMPLICATIONS OF TRIPS WITH SPECIAL REFERENCE TO HIGHER EDUCATION IN INDIA

R.Y. Mahore

The significance of Service Sector is increasing in the recent times. The services are intangible, invisible and perishables requiring simultaneous production and consumption. The share of services in world trade and investment has been increasing. The services have been among the fastest growing components if world trader since last 20 years.

The objective of this paper is to highlight the potential impact of trade liberalisation. The second objective is to raise questions and identify policy issues that require further attention and analysis. The current debate on this impact of GATS us rather polarised. The GATS is the first set of multilateral rules covering international trade in services. The WTO is the only global organisation dealing with the rules of trade between nations.

Article I of the GATS defines the scope of the Agreement and the nature of services trade. The GATS covers 12 sectors and 161 sub-sectors. The classified sectors are (1) Business (2) Communication (3) Construction (4) Distribution (5) Education (6) Environmental (7) Financial (8) Health (9) Tourism (10) Recreational (11) Transport and (12) Others.

GATS also in Article I define services trade as occurring through 4 modes of supply.

MODE 1: CROSS BORDER SUPPLY

The services are supplied from the territory one country into the territory of another country.

MODE 2: CONSUMPTION ABROAD

The services are supplied in the territory of the country to the consumer

MODE 3: COMMERCIAL PRESENCE

The services are supplied through any type of business of professional establishment of one member in the territory of another.

MODE 4: PRESENCE OF NATURAL PERSON

The services are supplied by national of one member in the territory of another. The GATS consists of three core elements:

1. General rules and principles governing trade in services,
2. Includes a series of annexes pertaining to regulatory principles agreed in specific service sector (air transport, financial services, maritime transport and telecommunications) and decisions on specific issues (movement of natural person).
3. Consist of schedules of commitments which outline the liberalisation of each member country. Sectoral schedule commitments concern market access and national treatment within designated sectors.

GATS AND HIGHER EDUCATION IN INDIA

The globalization of higher education in India has created problems of varied in nature. The globalisation would be desirable if it succeed in improving the educational standards without affecting the opportunities of others.

There are 5 categories of education services. These categories are based on United Nations Provisional Central Product classification and include:

(i) Primary education services,

(ii) Secondary education services,

(iii) Higher education services

(iv) Adult education services

(v) Other educational services

ASSESSING GATS COMMITMENTS IN EDUCATION SECTOR

The sectoral coverage of the many specific commitments on the market access and natural treatment that prevail in the GATS is limited. The developed countries have found it easier or more beneficial than the developing countries to submit relatively extensive schedules. The majority of the country schedules also list a variety of measures that continue to restrict market access or national treatment.

THE CONTROVERSIAL ISSUES RELATED TO HIGHER EDUCATION

The GATS is described as a voluntary agreement because countries can decide the sectors which will be covered under GATS rules. The question arises which education services are covered or exempted?

The Article 1.3 defines the services which are covered or exempted. The agreement is applied to all measures affecting services except, "those services supplied in the exercise of governmental authority". But what does, 'exercise of governmental authority mean'?

GATS supporters argue that the education provided and funded by the government is therefore exempted. According to critics more detailed analysis of the clause is necessary. As per agreement, "in the exercise of governmental authority" means the service is provided on a non-commercial basis and not in competition with other service suppliers. But what is meant by non-commercial basis and not in competition?" These are the core issues need more debate.

According to critics the public sector or government service providers would not be exempted. The situation is more complicated in those countries where there is a mixed system of higher education. The public as well as private institutions provide higher education services. A significant amount of funding for private institutions comes from the public sector.

Another implication is that a public institution in an exporting country is often defined as private or commercial when it crosses the border and delivers the services in the importing country. Therefore, it is necessary to understand the meaning of the term, "non-commercial", with reference to higher education trade.

The debate regarding 'not in competition' is also equally important. For example, if non-governmental providers (private non-profit or commercial) are delivering services, are they in competition with the government providers? In this case, public providers may be defined as being in 'competition' by the mere existence along with the private proiders.

Does the method of delivery influence the concept of 'in competition'? Does the term cover situations where there is a similar mode of delivery? Does this term mean that public providers using traditional face-to-face classroom methods could be seen to be competing with foreign profit e-learning providers?

There are many unanswered questions that need clarification. The supporters of the GATS argue that education is to a large extent a government function. The agreement does not seek to displace the public education system and the right of government to regulate and meet domestic policy objectives.

Critics emphasise that the protection of public services is very uncertain and potentially at risk. There is narrow interpretation of what governmental authority means and what 'not in competition' and non-commercial basis mean. All these problems must be debated at length.

In the case of education services in developing countries. fields such as medicine are often provided by government as subsidised rates along with private medical colleges. Do these satisfy the criteria under Article 1.3? Some infer that Article 1.3 lacks transparency.

The main problem to be solved is how to separate public and private participation under the GATS and development of objective criteria for this purpose. This question is related with the provision of subsidies in the education sector. The subsidy provision for education is related with the provision of subsidies in the education sector. The subsidy provision for education services plays an important role in addressing poverty alleviation, equity, social and distributional objectives in developing countries. The current GATS provisions for subsides do not prohibit their use. But the interpenetration of Article 1.3 could affect the use of subsidies in future. As a result, developing countries may need to defend against this possibility by retaining the right to use subsidies in their current commitments on national treatment.

The interpretation of Article VI is not clear regarding domestic regulation. The members have to regulate those services in which they have listed a commitment in a reasonable objective and impartial manner. Article VI also requires the countries to establish transparent domestic regulations that do not constitute unnecessary trade barriers. However, the meaning of the terms 'impartial', 'objective', 'reasonable' and 'unnecessary' trade barriers are not clarified anywhere in the GATS.

The GATS will not address the export interests in the education sector of many developing countries in the area of mode 4. The limited commitments that have made in mode 4 are subject to numerous market access and national treatment conditions, including quantitative restrictions on entry, economic needs tests, licensing and certification. The GATS therefore, offers limited potential to the developing countries to export labour based education services in which they may have comparative advantages.

WHAT DOES THE PRINCIPLE OF PROGRESSIVE LIBERALISATION MEAN?

GATS is not a neutral agreement. It aims to promote and enforce the liberalisation of trade in services. The process of progressive liberalisation involves two aspects:

(i) Extending GATS coverage to more service sectors and

(ii) Decreasing the number and extent of measures that serve as impediments to trade.

With each new round of negotiations, the countries are expected to add sectors or sub-sectors to their national schedule of commitments. They have to remove the limitations on market access and national treatment. If countries are not interested in the import or export of education services are likely to experience greater pressure to allow market access to foreign providers. GATS is very new instrument and it is too early to predict the potential opportunities or risks.

EFFECTS OF LIBERALISING EDUCATION TRADE ON DEVELOPING COUNTRIES:

The developing countries have to discuss the problems mentioned above and to shape the provisions suitable to their own interests. It is therefore, important for the developing countries to assess the potential costs and benefits of liberalising education services. The developing countries have to take necessary steps in order to avoid potential adverse consequences.

The developing countries are both exporters and importers of important educational services. Exports are mainly in the form of mode 2 and mode 4. Some of the more advanced developing countries in Asia and Latin America are providing educational services mode 1 through electronic delivery system. The imports of education services are mainly in the form of mode 2 and increasing via mode 3. There has been growing foreign involvement and collaboration in higher education services in developing countries in the recent years.

There are costs and benefits for the developing countries from the export promotion and import liberalisation of education services under each mode of supply. Mode 1 imports of education services through virtual education institutions could enable foreign education providers to cater to the needs of remote population at low cost. It is clear that mode 1 may not be cost effective for exporting and importing countries if information and communication technology infrastructure is lacking. There is also a risk that virtual learning may divert the government expenditure from basic education services and lead to concentration of technologies which satisfy the needs of few affluent.

Mode 2 has mixed implications. It may assist importing developing countries to overcome shortages of labour and capital. It may also help the exporting developing countries to improve their national education system by generating foreign exchange and resources for investment. It may create two tier structure in education system which crowd out the local population by creating a higher quality, expensive segment that cater to wealthy nationals and foreigners and a lower quality, resource, constrained section catering for the poor.

Mode 3 can benefit developing countries through investment of foreign capital in education systems. This reduces the burden on government resources and generates opportunities for domestic employment. These gains may be offset by the initial public investment that may be required to attract foreign investment. Internal brain-drain could occur as better quality education practitioners flow from the public education segment to the foreign segment which offers better pay and working conditions. This is also happening in India and also in Maharashtra. Some have left their previous jobs and joined institutions of international University.

As per mode 4, the increased mobility of education practitioners could generate remittances and transfer back to the exporting country, promote exchange of knowledge and help to upgrade skills and standards. The movement of educated personnel could provide an important means to overcome domestic shortages of labour and contain (wage) pressures in importing countries. If these outflows are permanent, they may lead to shortages of trained educated personnel in the exporting country and loss of public resources invested in their subsidised training or education.

The available evidence suggests that there had been a substantial increase in migration to the UAE during the first half of 1990s. But the situation has drastically changed since 1996. A large number of Indian migrants have forced to return to India due to the changes in the labour market and immigration policy of the UAE government. It is estimated that the volume of remittances from migrant workers from UAE to India was round Rs. 7200 crore in 2000. (Zuchariah: Prakash Irudaya Rajan, 2002). The major problem faced by several Indian emigrants in UAE are non-payment of salaries, denial of wages and non-wage benefits as per the contract, refusing to release the passport and non-payment of charges for air ticket to return to their native place. Therefore we can conclude that the validity of mode 4 is doubtful.

The developing countries need to asses their strength, and weaknesses in the education sector, the potential costs and benefits of liberalising these services and the role of domestic regulations. There is a need to clarify the scope of GATS under Article 1.3, to ensure subsidies under Article XIV remain exempt from the application of national treatment, to clarify for the meaning of Article VI on domestic regulation and to improve commitments on mode 4.

The main challenge for the developing countries is to balance the scope for increasing competition in education services under the GATS with the legitimate role of the governments to intervene and offset market failures and address social objectives.

POINTS FOR DISCUSSION

(i) The issue of transparency is most important: We do not know the country which has made offers of request. It is necessary to ask why should a country wish to commit education services to GATS?

(ii) It is said that most of the people are ignorant about the GATS and its possible implications for education. We have to think what governments want? We must also understand what is the providers interests. We have not heard about the wants of the students, their nature of demand, etc. Some argue that the export of expertise from rich countries to poor countries is a way of avoiding social disorder in rich countries. The most important question in developing countries is to identify their education needs.

(iii) All the people engaged in the debate on education and GATS have different perspectives. There are also diverse perspectives within the institutions. There are various reasons for importing and exporting education. There is little clarity on what the countries are actually doing.

(iv) The countries are making commitments in education which are not needed. U.N. agencies are asking why a country would want to do it.

(v) The suppliers of education services are targeting new, middle income economies than the low-income economies.

(vi) The trade led framework of GATS is different from UNESCO's framework. It is interesting to note that the same member states that are in the WTO are also in UNESCO. The motivations of WTO are mainly commercial whereas UNESCOs agenda is more cultural and right based.

(vii) The developed countries are talking about education and GATS in the context of profitability. Education is a right. GATS will make it a privilege. This contradicts the convention of Human Rights.

(viii) The WTO members have agreed to accept progressive liberalization. By minimising the scope of political interference in the economy, it is necessary to know who benefits from this set of rules. The US is adopting dual policy by liberalising export of education services on one side and regulating its own education market on the other side.

(ix) It is necessary to know the labour market situation. Otherwise labour will move out of a country and would be disappointed.

WHAT ARE THE IMPLICATIONS OF NEGOTIATIONS ACROSS SECTORS?

There are bilateral negotiations on market access and national treatment commitments. Some countries have not made commitments to open up education services to foreign providers. They need further clarification. There are other aspects of GATS, such as the dispute mechanism, subsidies, treatment of monopolies which are controversial and apply to all sectors need further study. It must be remembered that GATS is still an untested agreement and some confusion exists on how to interpret the major rules and obligations. It took many years to remove the inconsistencies of GATT and it may be true for GATS. It is necessary that the lawyers have to review the technical and legal aspects of the agreement. The educators need to study the application and impact of education services.

EXTENT OF COUNTRY COMMITMENTS

The education sector is one of the least committed sectors. Out of the WTO members only 44 have made commitments to education and only 21 of these have included commitments to higher education. Only 3 countries (U.S.A., New Zealand and Australia) have submitted a negotiating proposals mentioning their interests and issues In the proposals they have explained the role of government, purpose of trade liberalization, benefits of trade liberalisation and private/public mix etc.

FURTHER ANALYSIS REQUIRED

There are diverse perspectives on the number of commitments. The national objectives are different in various countries. Therefore, the goals and expectations from trade in education services are different. Some argue that there is a need to protect consumers by assuring appropriate levels of access and quality. Further debate and analysis is necessary regarding trade liberalisation.

ECONOMIC REFORMS AND FINANCING HIGHER EDUCATION IN INDIA

The quality and quantity of highly specialized human resources determine their competence in the global market. Emergence of knowledge as driving factor results in both challenges and opportunities. The percentage public expenditure upon higher education has been decreasing since 1991.

The higher education has been largely a state funded activity. The growth rates are doubled among the students enrolled in post graduate and research, while the number of institutions for post graduate and research studies has grown at a slower rate in 1990s than 1980s. The enrollment has been increasing in absolute terms, only 7 per cent of the population in the age group 17–24 attended higher educational institutions in India, as against 92% in U.S.A., 52% in U.K. and 45% in Japan.

The government and UGC are finding it difficult to sustain the current level of funding to the institutions of higher education. The Tenth Five Year Plan document notes that it is important to recognise that the universities must made greater efforts to supplement resources apart from the government. It is to be noted that higher education is no a longer a luxury, it is essential to national, social and economic development (UNESCO, 2000).

The adverse effect of economic reforms reflects upon various diversification measures such as hike in student fees, student loan programmes operated by commercial banks and privatisation. There are three important economic justification for government funding for higher education as:

(i) Higher education investments generate external benefits important for economic development, such as long-term return from basic research and technical development is essential for competition and globalization. Hence, public investment on higher education should enhance.

(ii) Private investment in higher education alone would be socially sub-optional.

(iii) The increased role of market undermines the participation of meritorious students form economically disadvantageous groups (World Bank, 1994).

COST RECOVERY MEASURES

The globalisation wave and the changes within the economic systems have forced the higher education system to opt for a number of cost recovery measures. The important cost recovery measures adopted in the Indian higher education system are student fees, students loans and privatisation.

STUDENT FEES

The government of India had constituted various committees to examine the issue of mobilization of resources for central universities (Under the chairmanship of Justice K. Punnayya, UGC, 1993) and for technical education (under the chairmanship of Dr. D. Swaminathan, AICTE, 1994). Another committees were constituted by UGC to specially look into the recommendations of Punnaya Committee on unit cost of higher education (under the chairmanship of M.V. Pylee, UGC, 1997) to review the norms of maintenance grants for Delhi colleges (under the chairmanship of Dr. Anandakrishnan, UGC, 1999) and to formulate the revision of fee structure (under the chairmanship of Dr. Mohhmmad-Ur Rehman, UGC, 2000). All these committees have recommended the upward revision of fees chargeable by universities and colleges from a reasonable to a substantial limit. It is recommended that certain monetary provisions be made to ensure that the revised fee structure being suggested by the committee is implemented (UGC, 2000, pp. 41-44 and 16).

With regard to fees for admission and examination, it is recommended to recover the recurring cost of operations. While library, laboratory, sports and similar other fees are concerned, it is suggested that these fees must be revised to recover a significant part of the recurring cost (UGC, 1993, p. 77). It is recommended to revise the development fee to meet the actual recurring cost on no-loss-no-profit basis (UGC, 1999–2000).

With economic reforms and other pressures on the government, higher education has been shifted to the list of non-merit good. It has been ignored that the expenditure on education is a social investment. The role of the state and the public support to higher education remains essential to ensure its educational, social and institutional goals.

STUDENT LOAN

The student loans are in operation in more than 100 countries around the world. Students loan programmes can safeguard the poor students from the rising cost of higher education. But due to lack of collateral security, the poor students can not borrow from education. There is a gradual shift from a regime of interest free loans to subsidies interest on student loans. The educational loan scheme was introduced in India following the announcement in the budget 2000–01. The world experience on student loans suggests that the recovery rate is very poor.

PRIVATISATION

The privatisation of higher education has emerged in several forms and types in the recent decade in India.

(i) Privatisation within government higher education institutions take place ion the form of introducing self financing courses.

(ii) Converting government aided private institutions into private institutions into private self financing institutions.

(iii) Allowing to expand self financing private institutions with recognition and also without recognition, which may be termed as commercial private higher education institutions.

The government of India in its Prime Minister's Council or Trade and Industry, appointed a committee to suggest reforms in the education sector, along with other sectors (headed by M. Ambani and K. Birla). It is strongly suggested for full cost recovery (user pays principle) from students even in public higher education institutions through hike in fees and introduction of self financing courses and seats, shifting of resources from higher education to primary education. The government should leave higher education completely to private sector. The committee also suggested that the user-pays principle be strictly enforced in higher education, supplemented by loans and grants to economically and socially backward sections of society (Ambani and Birla, 2001).

There are a number of important factors that led to emergence and rapid expansion of private higher education in India. They are classified as pull and push factors. In addition to these, the external factors are also responsible for the growth of private higher education.

Pull Factors—The Conventional universities are not able to cater to the demands of new sections of population for higher education. A nexus between academics and industry is met by private institutions with multi disciplinary or inter disciplinary courses. These private institutions marketed their service technology courses varying from hi-tech to fashion technology. The management courses ranging from instructional management to hotel management and promised to produce not only employable youth but also to place them in jobs.

Push Factors—These factors include reduced allocation to higher education, introduction of cost-recovery measures within public institutions and directed policy measures toward privatisation of higher education Another important factor is the deteriorating quality of higher education in the country.

External factors—In the phase of internationalising higher education, foreign universities have been allowed to come to India and establish franchise centres in the country. It is to be noted that the private institutions in developing countries like India are not efficient, competitive as found in developed countries.

CONCLUSIONS

It is important that the self-financing courses are short term in nature and will have repercussions on the equity, balance and quality of education system in the long run. The increasing reliance on student fees, student loans and privatisation without considering the low income groups may produce regressive effects in the society.

The challenge to public on higher education in India is to combine provide providers with continuing responsibility of governments to guide, regulate, monitor and continuing the provision of subsidised higher education with a view to strike a balance between equality and efficiency principles.

THE INTEREST OF DEVELOPING COUNTRIES

The voices and interests of developing countries differ. The quality and accreditation are at the heart of much debate. The agreement focuses on temporary migration of labour force but it may lead to permanent migration. It will be a major challenge to improve education system if well qualified professionals are attracted in other countries. The poor countries are removing barriers while rich countries retain barriers on certain goods. Therefore, some developing countries have expressed strong reactions about the impact of GATS.

It must be mentioned that some countries have not made any financial commitments to trade in higher education services, but are removing trade barriers. The number of countries are changing visa and employment requirements to attract more international students. Students visa is not required in Canada for courses of under 6 months duration.

It is reported that 1.21 lakh Indian students were studying in 7 countries during 2003–04. The percentage of Indian students to total international students in USA was 13.9. They roughly contribute $ 2 billion to America. About 54.3 per cent more Indian students were admitted in Australia as compared to 2002–03. On the contrary, the enrolment in New Zealand decreased by 25.9 per cent. The decrease in number is mainly attributed to the changes in the New Zealand immigration policy in early 2004.

It is important not to overstate or understate the potential implications of GATS. One must be liberal while considering exporting opportunities and more protectionist when analysing the implications of importing. There are challenges and opportunities to the Indian education system from globalisation. The challenges are more dominant than opportunities. Public support for higher education remains essential to ensure balance between the educational and social goals.

REFERENCES

Ambani, M. and Birla, K. (2001), "Report on a Policy Framework for Reforms in Education", Government of India, New Delhi.

Government of India (1992), "Programme of Action on the National Education Policy, Ministry of Human Resource Development", New Delhi.

Government of India (1997), "Approach paper to the Ninth Five Year Plan: 1997–2002, Planning Commission, New Delhi.

Government of India (2001), "Approach paper to the Tenth Five Year Plan: 2002–2007, Planning Commission, New Delhi.

Government of India (1997–2002), Ninth Five Year Plan: 1997–2002, Planning Commission, New Delhi.

Government of India (2002–2007), Tenth Five Year Plan: 2002–2007, Planning Commission, New Delhi.

Rani, Geetha P. (2002), "Financing Higher Education in India during the Post Reform Period: Focus on Access and Equity", NIEPA Occasional Paper, No. 31, NIEPA, New Delhi, September, 2002.

______Rani, Geetha P. (2003), "Financing Higher Education in India in Economic Reform Period: Focus on Intra Sectoral Allocation of Resources to Education", in Globalisation and Challenges of Education, (ed.) NIEPA.

Srivastava, D.K. and Tapas K. Sen (1997), "Government Subsidies in India", National Institute of Public Finance and Policy, New Delhi.

Tilak J.B.G. (2001), "Education and Globalisation: The Changing Concerns in Economics of Education" (ed.), Perspectives in Education, Vol. 17, Special Issues, pp. 5–8.

Knight Jane (2002), "Trade in Higher Education Service: The Implications of GATS", The Observatory on Borderless Higher Education, U.K.

UNESCO(2002), "Education Today: Higher Education for Sale", The Newsletter of UNESCO, Education Sector, Paris.

Rose Pauline (2003), "Education and the General Agreement on Trade in Services: What does the Future Hold?, The Commonwealth Secretariat, London.

UGC (2000), "Report of the Committee Constituted by UGC for Formulation of Revised Fee Strcuture in the Central and Deemed Universities in India", UGC, New Delhi.

World Bank (1994), "Higher Education: Lessons from Experience", Washington D.C.

Candice Zachariah (2005), Class Apart: Indian 'Wizards' Prefer the land of OZ', Economic Times, Tuesday 1st February, 2005.

WTO (1998), Education Services, Background note by the Secretarian Council for Trade in Services, Geneva, Switzerland, S/C/W/49, 98–3691.

Cunningham S et.al., (2000), "The Business of Borderless Education, Department of Education, Training and Youth Affairs, Canberra, Australia.

Nauryal, D.K. and Bhalla, S. (2004), "Higher Education in the New Millennium: The need for a Paradigm Shift", Journal of Educational Planning and Administration, 17 (3rd July).

Kaushik, Madhulika (2004), GATS and Cross Boarder Supply (Mode I) in Higher Education: Strategies and Implications', Paper presented in the National Conference of Internationalisation of Higher Education Issues and Corners, New Delhi, August 26 and 27.

Power, K.B. (2004), "Domestic Regulation Relating to Foreign Providers of Higher Education in India", Paper presented in the National Conference of Internationalisation of Higher Education Issues and Corners, New Delhi, August 26 and 27.

Riley, Maria (2002), "Education Matters: General Agreement on Trade in Services (GATS) International Gender and Trade Network Secretariat.

Reddy, S. Surendranath (2004), "Trade in Educational Service, Globalisation of Education by WTO and GATS: The challenges and Opportunities to Indian Education", paper Submitted in the International Conference Organised by NIRMA, Ahmedabad on Trade, Technology and Environment.

Chanda R. (2003), "General Agreement on Trade in Services", Economic and Political Weekly, April 19.

Prasad H.A.C. (2003), "WTO talks on Services and Export Prospects", Financial Express, August 28.

9

AGENDA FOR MAHARASHTRA'S TEXTILE INDUSTRY

P.R. Wadjé

The Textile Industry including Cotton, Silk, Woollen, Jute and Man-made fibres is Prime Industry in India on many counts. It consists of the orgnised mill sector, traditional handloom sector and decentralised powerloom Sector. It is one of the oldest and second largest employment-oriented industry next only to agriculture. This oldest traditional and essential industry is not only meeting the essential cloth requirements of India but also earning fabulous foreign exchange. Thus this industry has a vital role to play in the nation's economy. The industry is substantially developed and became complex with hand spinning and hand weaving sector at the one end and the modern mechanised mill sector at the other. In between, fall the decentralised small scale powerlooms.

The Handloom industry mainly comprises of 3 Sectors: (1) Cotton Weaving (2) Wool weaving and (3) Silk weaving. Out of the three, cotton weaving accounts for about 90% of the weaving activity in terms of number of handlooms. Handloom industry is the source of livelihood for the largest number of Indians. There are over 30 lakh handlooms (Cotton) that provide employment to about 100 lakh people on weaving along.

India has the third largest technological and skilled man power in the world. It has the second largest consumer market consisting of more than 220 million middle income people. The land under cotton cultivation in India is around one fourth of the total land under cotton cultivation in the world. It's textile history runs back to seventh century. It is therefore ironical that India has an insignificant share of around 4% in the world textile trade. India continues to operate at the bottom end of the price line in the world textile trade. It has failed to capture the world textile market for high value added materials.

It is worth noting that China, Hongkong, South Korea and Taiwan have registered their presence significantly in the world textile market through conscious efforts. While they continued to globalise their textile economy. The industry has witnessed significant growth during the last decade in terms of installed spindleage, production of yarn (both spun-filament), output of cloth and its per capita availability as also exports. Thus, the number of Cotton/man-made fibre textile mills (which comprise the cotton yarn, blended yarn and other spun yarn manufacturing units and the compositive units) rose from 1142 in 1993 to 1875 by the end of March, 2003. The growth has been entirely due to increase in Spinnning mills which rose from 874 in 1993 to 1599 units by March, 2003, with the spinning capacity increasing from 28 million spindles to 36 million spindles during the same period, registering an addition of 8 lakh spindles per annum. After the announcement of the liberalised industrial policy in July, 1991 and the issuance of the 'Textile (Development and Regulation) Order, 1993 the pace of setting up of textile spinning mills has increased. The growth of the spinning sector has been characterised by the installation of more rotors in this decade (which now number about 3.79 lakh) and coming up of Export Oriented units (EOUs), mainly for the production of cotton yarn, and such units now stood at 93.

The growth in the composite mill Sector has been stagnating almost since independence. The total number of composite mills, which was 276 in 1951 rose marginally to 291 in the year 1971 and declined to 266 in 1994. Since then it has again marginally increased to reach 276 in 2003. The weaving capacity of the organised mill sector stagnated for a number of years, largely because the government policy permitted only a marginal expansion in the weaving capacity of the organised mill sector. Even after the removal of the restrictions on the creation of capacities the Textile Policy of June, 1985, the Weaving Capacity has consistently been declining since 1988. Between 1993 and 2003, the weaving capacity has decreased annually at 3 per cent. This is compensated by emergence of decentralised powerloom and hosiery sectors in a bigway.

The Indian Textile Industry has natural advantages of strong multi-fibre base traditional skills and cheap labour, these strengths get diluted due to high contamination of cotton, lack of technology, upgradation, low productivity, an absence of focussed and co-ordinated development strategy, inadequate product diversification and value addition and an inability to meet the quality and market compliance. As a result, its global market share continues to stagnate at around 4%, although there has been an increase in absolute numbers.

The *SSIs/SMEs form the backbone of Indian textile industry (except in spinning) and any strategy of strengthening the Indian Textile Industry should invariably focus on the capacity building of these SMEs.

Another features of the Indian textile industry is in terms of location of the SMEs in defined clusters. Various clusters, across the country, have emerged for identifiable activities over a period of time. For example, the powerloom activity is concentrated in clusters like Surat, Bhiwandi, Ichalkaranji, Malegaon, Erode, Salem and Burhanpur, the knitwear activity has clustered in and around Ludhiana and Tirupur, Kannur, Karur and Panipat have emerged as home furnishing clusters, Bangalore, Chennai and Delhi are emerging as apparel manufacturing clusters, Guntar and Indore are the known clusters for cotton ginning and pressing activity, Coimbatore and Madhurai are known cotton spinning clusters; there are numerous handloom clusters in every part of the country. The SMEs located in these clusters share common threats and opportunities.

The onset of globalisation of trade and economic liberalisation within the country has posed new challenges and opportunities

*SSI: Small Scale Industry. SME: Small Medium Enterprise.

fro the Indian textile industry. As part of Agreement on Textiles and clothing (ATC) under the WTO frame work, all the quantitative restriction (quotas) on imports and exports has ceased to exist from January 1, 2005. Such integration of markets will provide several opportunities as well as threats to Indian textile industry. It is an opportunity since the market access is unlimited and unrestricted. It is a threat since minimum assured quantities, hitherto available for exports under quotas are not available. In such a highly competitive environment, only those companies with strong fundamentals and conscious to several market compliances and price, alone can survive. Apart from integration of markets without any quotas the WTO framework demands the gradual phasing out of non-compatible (to the WTO agreement) protections, currently available to the industry, in the form of subsidies and other incentives. The Indian industry will also have to guard its domestic market share, in addition to consolidatign and enlarging the expert market share.

Therefore, the Indian textile industry will have to look for competing and surviving purely on its strength and competitive edge. A comprehensive strategy, involving the Government and industry partnership is the need of the hour to convert the threats into opportunities and, sustain and enlarge our domestic and international market shares.

CHALLENGES IN INDIAN TEXTILES

The first challenge is the scalability of operations while the total size of the industry is around Rs. 140,000 crores comprising of Rs. 52,000 crores of exports there are hardly 2 or 3 companies clocking a turnover of 2000 crores. This shows the fragmented nature of the industry compared to international standards our capacities are small. For example in the Spinning Sector, a capacity of 1, 00, 000 Spindles is considered as large in India. But compared to international standards this capacity is small to average. In China for example, a capacity of 3 lakh Spindles is quite common there are units which are as large as one million spindles or 10 lakhs. Similarly, in the weaving processing and garment sectors our capacities are miniscule compared to international standards. In

China and Shrilanka the average machine per garment factories is 500 compared to 50 in India.

The second biggest Challenge facing the industry is the supply chain management. It is estimated that by 2010, more than 25% of the world's textile trade will be controlled by retail giants. In such a scenario an efficient supply chain management cannot be over emphasized. The retail giants will determine the export prices and only an efficient supply chain will be able to compete effectively. In fact it will be competition between supply chain and not between companies. There are hardly any companies in India having a presence in the entire textile chain from yarn to garments.

The third challenge facing the industry is the effective integration of the various sectors of the textile industry. For more than 25 years the various wings of the industry like the powerloom, handloom, mill sector, knitted garments, woven garments have been competing with each other for fiscal insentives and duty concessions. Now that a level playing field has been brought about the role of each sector has to be clearly defined while the powerloom sector can cater to the mass market in the domestic sector for the lower and mid sections of the society, with of course the exception of some modernized units at the Apparel parks etc. The mill sector could be allowed to take over garments units and cater to the export sector and upper end of the market in the domestic market.

The Fourth Challenge facing the industry relates to moving up the value chain. There are two dimensions when it comes to moving us the value chain one relates to what China did. China consciously decided that they will export value added products instead of exporting yarn, the highest value being in garments China's share in Global Textile Trade is 13.5% and in Global Clothing Trading is 20.6% amounting to 20.56 Billion US $ and 41.30 Billion US $ respectively. While this may hurt some of the sectors adversely in the short run over an extended period of time, this will be beneficial to the entire industry. This could also give filling to the developments of weaving and processing sectors which at present are the weak links in the textile value chain. The other dimension of moving up the value chain relates to the higher end of the market. A majority of exports of garments cater to the lower end of the value chain. The industry needs to move up to the middle and higher end, where the value realizations are much higher.

The next challenge facing the industry is improvement in the crop yield of cotton, while we boast of availability of all the varieties of cotton, our yields are one of the lowest in the world and in consistent in quality. Enough attention had not been paid to the modernization of the ginning sector in the past.

Yet another challenge facing the industry relates to the management structure. Most of the textile units are family managed. In order to overcome the various challenges outlined here and as a measure of good corporate governance, ownership needs to be diverted and distinct from management control. We have seen this trend taking roots in other industries but textiles being an industry having presence in both the organized as well as the unorganized sectors. There are good owner managers of spinning sectors but to accelerate growth and vertically integrate to value addition and economics of scale professionalism is the need of the hour.

COTTON

The cotton branch of the textile industry has increased at such a rate during the last Century in all parts of the Wrold, and has now arrived at such proportions, that it may safely be said to occupy the foremost position among the industrial arts. It has more money invested in buildings, plants and stock and employs more work people, directly and indirectly, than any other manufacturing branch of trade in this or probably any other country. It is supposed that the manufacture of cotton originated in India about 1100 B.C., and the methods then used have practically remained the same, until within a comparatively recent date.

In the growth of the textile industry in the country, cotton has played a crucial role. Cotton is still the predominant fibre used in the Textile Sector. However, there has been continuous decline in terms of share in consumption of cotton. The share of cotton in the consumption to total fibre by the industry that was 71 per cent in 1992–93 has now declined to 55 per cent. However, in absolute terms the consumption of cotton has increased over the period from 1895 million kgs. in 1992–93 to 2699 million kgs. in 2002–03. The

Table 1
Textiles in India

Items	*Unit*	*1998–99*	*1999–00*	*2000–01*	*2001–02*	*2002–03 Provisional*
Cotton/Man made Fibre Textiles Mills	No.	1824	1850	1846	1860	1875
Spinning Mills (Non-SSI)	No.	1543	1565	1565	1579	1599
Composite Mills (Non-SSI)	No.	281	285	281	281	276
Spinning Mills (SSI)	No.	901	921	996	1046	1146
Exclusive weaving Mills (Non-SSI)	No.	199	202	203	207	209
Powerloom units	Lakh No.	3.58	3.67	3.74	3.75	3.80
Capacity Installed						
Spindle (SSI + Non-SSI)	Million No.	36.67	37.08	37.91	38.33	39.02
Rotors (SSI + Non -SSI)	Lakh No.	4.34	4.44	4.54	4.80	4.69
Looms (Organised sector)	Lakh No.	1.40	1.40	1.40	1.41	1.37
Powerlooms	Lakh No.	15.99	16.30	16.62	16.66	16.92
Handloom	Lakh No.	38.91	38.90	38.91	38.91	38.91
Man-made fibres	Million kg.	1064	1066	1081	1090	1096
Man-made filaments	Million kg.	1033	1078	1128	1135	1190
Worsted spindles (Woollen)	Thousand No.	575	585	598	598	604
Non-worsted spindles (Wollen)	Thousand No.	412	419	426	426	437

Contd....

Items	*Unit*	*1998–99*	*1999–00*	*2000–01*	*2001–02*	*2002–03 Provisional*
Production Fibres						
Raw Cotton	Lakh bales	165.00	156.00	140.00	158.00	136.00
Man-made fibres	Million kg.	782	835	904	834	914
Raw wool	Million kg.	48.33	46.50	47.00	47.00	47.00
Raw silk	Million kg.	15.54	15.21	15.86	17.35	16.21
Production Yarn						
Cotton yarn	Million kg.	2022	2204	2267	2212	2177
Other spun yarn	Million kg.	786	842	893	889	904
Man-made filament yarn	Million kg.	850	894	920	962	1100
Production of Fabric						
Cotton	Million Sq. Mtr.	17948	18989	19718	19769	19300
Blended	Million Sq. Mtr.	5700	5913	6351	6287	5876
100% Non-cotton (including Khadi, Wool & Silk)	Million Sq. Mtr.	12479	14306	14164	15978	16797
Total	Million sq. Mtr.	36127	39208	40233	42034	41973
Per Capita availability of cloth	Sq. mtr.	28.19	30.55	30.68	31.97	31.37
Production of Textile Machinery	Million US $	270.32	256.70	286.90	225.64	243.48
Textile Exports (Including Jute, Coir & Handicraft)	Million US $	9546.99	10521.37	12129.47	10797.53	12501.52
Textile Imports	Million US $	851.14	1128.59	1172.40	1537.10	1645.82

import of cotton has been negligible as compared to the total consumption in a year but increased substantially during 1999–2000 due to the poor quality and high price of the domestic cotton. During 2002–03 the import constituted 11 per cent of cotton consumption. However, the export of cotton varied depending on the size of the Cotton Crop. The demand for cotton from mills has increased significantly due to the expansion in the consuming industry.

The prices of raw cotton, the main fibre for the textile industry ruled at higher level during 2002–03 than that in 2001–02. The weighted average price of raw cotton was 41.2 per cent higher in March, 2003, as compared to March 2002. During the last five years period i.e., March 1998 to March 2003, the weighted average price, however, declined marginally by 3.4 per cent. In terms of compounded annual rate of growth (CARG), the raw cotton prices declined by 0.7 per cent during the last five years.

The weighted average price of cotton hank yarn increased by 15.7 per cent between March, 2002 and 2003. The price of cone yarn also increased by 6.6 per cent during the above period. The price of hosiery cone yarn however declined marginally by 1.4 per cent. During last five years period i.e., March, 1998 to March, 2003 the price of hank yarn and hosiery cone yarn increased by 9.8 per cent and 0.7 per cent respectively. However, the price of cone yarn declined by 2.0 per cent. In terms of compounded annual rate of growth (CARG), the prices of hank yarn and hosiery cone yarn were increased by 1.9 per cent and 0.1 per cent respectively during the last five years. However, for cotton cone yarn the same is declined by 0.4 per cent.

The cotton yarn has the dominant share which accounted for 81 per cent of the total spun yarn production for the year 1992–93. Its share has been declining in the recent years and during 2002–03, its share was 71 per cent of the total spun yarn production in the country, while the remaining 29 per cent was in the form of blended and 100% non-cotton yarn. The trend in the production of cotton yarn in the past had fluctuated in tandem with the cotton crop in different years. On an average, during the last 10 years or so, the trend of production of cotton yarn has shown an increase of

Table 2
Textile Industry in Maharashtra Textiles in India

Items	*Unit*	*1998–99*	*1999–00*	*2000–01*	*2001–02*	*2002–03 Provisional*
Cotton/Man made Fibre Textiles Mills	No.	201	205	207	207	209
Spinning Mills (Non-SSI)	No.	124	128	130	129	131
Composite Mills (Non-SSI)	No.	77	77	77	78	78
Spinning Mills (SSI)	No.	11	11	12	15	15
Exclusive Weaving Mills (Non-SSI)	No.	68	69	69	70	71
100% Export oriented Units (EOUs)	No.	17	18	17	18	19
Powerloom units	No.	175135	178402	183459	183837	188268
Man-made fibre units	No.	5	5	5	5	5
Man-made filament yarn units	9	9	9	9	9	9
No of power processing units	No	249	N.A.	N.A.	N.A.	N.A.
Capacity Installed						
Spindle (SSI + Non-SSI)	Thousand No.	5043	5166	5212	5218	5173
Rotors (SSI + Non-SSI)	No.	43860	44364	45972	46572	47212
Looms (Composite & Exclusive weaving units)	No.	42317	41732	41203	41227	41504
No. of Powerlooms	No.	672102	692603	707145	709438	730945
Manmade fibre	Mn.kg.	246.75	246.75	244.95	244.95	246.75
Man-made filaments	Million kg.	281.30	281.30	306.30	302.70	325.80
Workers on Roll						
Spinning Mills & Composite Mills (Non-SSI)	No.	176918	178782	180541	180926	180682
Spinning Mills (SSI)	No.	723	723	854	1084	1010
Exclusive weaving mills (Non-SSI)	No.	8199	5794	5982	5997	6199
EOUs	No.	5844	6885	7075	7630	7853
Production Fibres						
Raw Cotton	Lakh bales	26.50	38.00	20.50	33.50	26.00
Man-made fibres	Thousand kg.	226360	236971	253959	252427	263699
Cotton Consumption by Mills						
Non-SSI						

Items	*Unit*	*1998–99*	*1999–00*	*2000–01*	*2001–02*	*2002–03 Provisional*
SSI	Thousand kg.	1992	3545	4275	5348	5818
Production Yarn						
Cotton yarn	Thousand kg.	268386	272069	271961	251325	234901
Blended yarn	Thousand kg.	79038	81434	75332	66627	62806
100% Non-cotton yar	Thousand kg.	6977	9026	14498	20640	26413
Total Spun Yarn	Thousand kg.	354401	362529	361791	338592	324120
Man-made filament yarn	Thousand kg.	270728	279388	293803	308254	352517
Fabric Production (Mill Sector)						
Cotton	Thousand Sq. Mtr.	495024	513499	497408	419026	382257
Blended	Thousand Sq. Mtr.	197088	161991	113708	81134	64232
100% Non-cotton	Thousand Sq. Mtr.	297	2869	3162	125	822
Total	Thousand Sq. Mtr.	692409	678359	614278	500285	447311
Closure position (Non-SSI)						
Spinning	No.	16	23	31	31	31
Composite	No.	10	11	12	16	17
Total	No.	26	34	43	47	48
Affected due to closure						
Spindles	Thousand No.	775	941	1116	1286	1319
Rotors	No.	2616	3360	4528	4888	4898
Looms	No.	6451	7699	7734	9998	10648
Workers on roll	No.	34248	38226	47399	55026	56272
TUFS						
No. of applications received	No.	–	21	49	79	174
Total cost of project	Rs. crore	–	3672.74	1711.01	2027.44	2552.84
No. of application sanctioned	No.	–	13	31	60	148
Amount sanctioned	Rs. crore	–	224.41	357.05	471.42	751.05
No. of application disbursed	No.	–	5	20	48	111
Amount disbursed	Rs. crore	–	55.70	234.05	339.94	515.12

3 per cent per annum. The production of cotton yarn had fluctuated in the year 1991–92, 1994–95, 1998–99, 2001–02 and 2002–03 such fluctuations in the production of cotton yarn had also affected the total availability of spun yarn and to a certain extent.

The cotton textiles have generally been contributing significantly towards the export earnings (its share being 27 per cent). The garments segment accounted for 46 per cent of the total textile exports during 2002–03. The trade in garments has grown not only in value terms but there has also been a remarkable diversification in the range of products and the direction of exports to different countries. The share of man-made fibre textile which was 7.5 per cent in 1998–99 now accounts for 11.4 per cent in total textile exports. The export of woolen textiles which accounted for 0.8 per cent during 1998–99 has now declined to 0.4 per cent.

COTTON TEXTILE INDUSTRY IN MAHARASHTRA

Textile industry remains the mainstay in Maharashtra. Both Mill and decentralised sector are concentrated in the state. Thus the textile industry is region specific, Ichalkaranji, Bhiwandi, Malegaon are major textile centres in Maharashtra.

Are the strengths appropriate to leverage on the opportunities that beckon? What do we need to do to overcome our weaknesses and combat the looming threats that might evade us from achieving our milestones? We take a quick look at the SWOT Analysis of the Maharashtra's Textile Industry.

SWOT ANALYSIS OF MAHARASHTRA'S TEXTILE INDUSTRY

Strength

- Existence of more than sufficient productive capacity.
- Easy vailability of skilled labour.
- Managements with business background.
- Presence of qualified technical personnel's from state's institute itself.
- Comfortable availability of raw meterials.

- Large domestic market.
- Material and machinery available for many of the products.
- Avility to run short batches.
- Availability of testing facilities.

Weakness

- Low level of modernisation and upgradation of technology.
- Low level of productivity due to inadequate formal training.
- Horizontal growth of powerlooms (SME's).
- No exposure to export markets.
- Difficulties in accessing of testing designing and technical services.
- Resigned attitude of managements due to recent setbacks.
- Cost based market set up.
- Not ready for diversification of products.
- No willingness to change existing work practices.
- No access to market information/inadeqate market information.

Opportunities

- Growing domestic and international markets.
- Untapped markets in Latin America and other countries also.
- Product mix and product diversification.
- Becoming sub-contractor to large units.
- Catering to bulk orders by distributing the work over the cluster units to form networks.
- Abundant scope to supply to multinationals shops setting up in India.
- Forming of raw material consortium/Raw material bank.

Threats

- Entry of multinational in domestic markets.

- Stiff competition from other countries (The performance of global competitor's in fabrics and garments indicates that there are at least 4 countries i.e., China, Indonesia, Thailand and Pakistan).
- Non-tariff barriers from developing countries.
- Slow improvement in quality to international standards and adoption to fast changing fashion demands.

THE AGENDA FOR THE MAHARASHTRA'S TEXTILE INDUSTRY COULD BE ON THE FOLLOWING LINES

Benchmarking Performance

Enterprises need to develop a mechanism to compare performance with competitors in other countries. Benchmarking with most efficient producers on all cost parameters is a must to improve the performance and remain competitive in the globalised scenario.

Better Value Chain Management

Improved value chain managemnet can reduce costs and increase flexibility. A wide sourcing base can increase flexibility when it comes to securing raw material from the cheapest source with the quality and design the buyer expects. Such flexibility will be a critical competitive factor in the future. By optimizing the supply chain, lead time will also be reduced.

Increase Productivity

Investment in human capital and high tech machinery to increase productivity and production of Internationally cost and quality competitive goods.

Quality Consciousness

To survive in the integrated world market, the industry has to focus on the internal standards of quality and excellence. To achieve internationally comparable and quality standard finished goods, it has to be ensured that quality parameters are maintained at each level of production from raw material to the finished product.

Modern Management Practices

Along with technology upgradation, adoption of modern management practices is also very essential to acquire that essential competitive edge. Management practices like JIT, TQM, supply chain management etc. from and important link between technology adoption and acquisition of competitiveness, Adoption of such practices will result in cut down in manufacture and delivery lead time, improving product and process quality and improving plant and equipment maintenance. Management accountability through stricter code of corporate governance is also necessary for balance corporate growth.

Distinctive Capabilities

The 'Mantra' for survival of textile units in the globalized economy will be to have distinctive capabilities. Each of the textile units, irrespective of the segments they are operating in, will necessarily have to develop distinctive capabilities and identity around which its growth can be centered. Textile units will also have to identify their areas of strengths and core competence to focus on such areas only vacating areas in which they are vulnerable to the threat of import penetration.

Innovative Products

The industry has to focus on innovation for surviving the stiff international competition. 'Production innovation' should be considered as a dynamic process and not as a one time process. Continuous innovation in the product is the sure way to win the race in the global market.

Develop 'e-application'

E-applications can be employed not only to sell, but also to exchange information across electronic networks at any stage of the supply chain. E-applications facilitate sourcing and supply chain management, production planning, design and forward integration, including Internet Sales. The main goal

AGENDA FOR MAHARASHTRA GOVT

Maharashtra Government needs to develop a strategic approach to tackle with the challenges of the quota free textile market. The action plan has to be based on partnership of government and the industry. The government has to provide conductive policy environment to strengthen the fundamentals of the industry, while industry has to formulate its action plan at the micro level for achieving international competitiveness.

The Agenda for the Maharashtra Government Could be on the Following Lines

1. Attracting foreign investments by display of potential.
2. Develop an organisation, which will be offering quality training programmes continuously in the area of Export and Import Market, product development, Total Quality Management, to the decentralized textile centres in Maharashtra.
3. State Government should make availability of continuous power supply to the Industry.

What the Maharashtra's Textile Industry should Aim to Achieve?

Several aspects have come to the lime light that we as the Maharashtra's Textile Industry should focus upon. The responsibility lies with many, both within, allied to and outside the gamut of Textile. With a clear vision of the key levers of success, strategic Intent is required. The activities for success include the Government, Industry Associations and the organizations.

The Maharashtra's Textile Industry should aim to become the most preferred and competitive textile hub for global sourcing. This can be achieved through a strategy called out from leveraging the strengths and opportunities and combating the weaknesses and challenges.

CONCLUSION

The Textile Industry in Maharashtra State in one of the few industries which has the potential to emerge as a true global player. A well-devised action plan coupled with effective delivery mechanism can see Maharashtra is emerging as a winner in the quota free market.

REFERENCES

UNCTAD Secretariat (1994), "Market-Trends and commodity Development for Cotton", 7th January.

"Export prospects of Cotton Fabrics to select Markets", (1994), Ashish Shrivastava, MPIB (1992–94), IIFT.

World Bank Publication (1992), "The Uruguay Round Textile Trade and the Developing Countries: Eliminating the MFA in the 1990s" (ed.) by by Carl B. Hamilton.

Exports/Imports data-Source-DGCI and S., Kolkata.

South India Cotton Association: Keynote Address by G.K. Sundaram (8th May, 1994).

"Khanna's International Trade in Textiles, (1991), MFA Quotas and a Developing Exporting Country", Sage Publications, New Delhi.

Consumber Purchases of Textiles-2002, Part -I (Textile Committee).

"India's Textile Trade Threats and opportunites" by Dr. R. Mandal and M.S. Verma, Economic Times.

"Disease Management Technology in Cotton" by Sheo Raj and P.K. Chakrabartty, Central Institute for Cotton Research.

"Present Status and future Thrusts in Cotton Prodution in India" (7th May, 1994) by C.H. Mirani, Welcome Address.

Directorate of Economics and Statistics, Ministry of Agriculture and Cotton Advisory Board.

Hand book of Textiles by A.F. Barker published by Abhishek Publication SCO 57–59, Sector 17–C, Chandigarh –160017.

The Standard Handbook of Textiles by A.J. Hall published by Butter Worth and Co. (Publishers) Ltd., London: 88 Kingsway, WC2B6AB.

Indian Textiles An Intersectoral perspective edited by S.S. Mehta and Vinod Shanbhag Published by Oxford & IBH Publishing Co. Pvt. Ltd. New Delhi.

Industrial Sickness, The Challenge in Indian Textiles Edited by V.Padaki & V.Shanbhag. Published by R.C. Vora for ATIRA, P.O. Polytechnic, Ahmedabad-380015.

Rehabilitation of the Textile Industry Edited and Executed by ATIRA, A Joint Publication of ATIRA, BTRA, SITRA & NITRA.

Census of Handlooms (1987–88).

The Textiles (Woes and Echoes of An Ailing Industry) by Madan Gaur Published by P.P.S.I. Colaba, Bombay-400039

India's Textile Industry (A Socio-Economic Analysis) by Kasthuri Sreenivasan Published by SITRA Coimbatore-641014

Indian Textile Industry in International Perspective by K.S.V. Menon Published by Current Awareness Service Bombay. 1980

History of the Indian Cotton Textile Industry by V.K. Kulkarni Published by R.L.N. Vijayanagar. The Secretary, The Millowner's Association, Bombay-400023.

Compendium of Textile Statistics, 2003.

Website: www.hometextileonline.com.

Website: www.texprocil.com.

Website: www.pdexcil.org.

Website: texmin.nic.in

Website: txcindia.com.

10

COMMENTS AND OBSERVATIONS ON TECHNICAL SESSION ON AGENDA FOR INDUSTRIES AND SERVICES SECTOR

J.F. Patil

In this session three papers, one each on infrastructure, textile industry and higher education were presented by Dr. Basawaraj, Prof. Wadje and Prof. R.Y. Mahore respectively.

Dr. Basvaraj examines the total infrastructure profile of the state of Karnataka against the general background of globalization. He pointed out the financial mess in which most of the states public undertaking are found and attributes the major discredit for the state level fiscal derailment experienced in the recent past to this mess for improving fiscal health of the state government, according to Dr. Basavaraj, it is imperative that tax revenues are increased, non tax revenues are increased and public expenditure of unproductive and socially irrelevant nature controlled. He discusses in great details various components of infrastructure like power, water, transport, public work department, as also urban systems.

Dr. Basavaraj's presentation throws up directly and indirectly a series of questions related to issues connected with privatization of infrastructure activities on the lines of guidelines given by international agencies. In this connection one fundamental question needs to be raised as to wether components of infrastructure of the nature of public utilities be given to the private sector? What about strategic consideration? In this connection the most important principle to kept mind is policy making in the light of Indian socio-economic realities and the needs and aspirations of the Indian people. In this frame work, the future development of infrastructure facility in the states will have to be with reference to ownership, management, technology up-gradation, and role of private/foreign investment. The most critical part in respect of infrastructure facility is related to objective and economic pricing and as and where required, equally objective subsidy targeting to minimize subsidy burden on the budget. It is felt that at least for the next decade two or power, irrigation, transport, urban amenities and education as well as health will have to be the responsibility of the government if the development is to be equitable in terms of regions and various sections of population.

Prof. Wadje paper on Agenda for Maharashtra Textile Industry quite informative and rich in data. It gives a general picture of Indian textile industries and spells out the various attributes of Indian textile industry highlighting major role played by small and medium enterprises. He explains the challenges of globalization for Indian textile industry. He rightly points out that Indian textile industry is largely fragmented with limitation like low quality cotton, low cotton yield, high cost per unit of cloth because of obsolete machinery, limitations of production of machinery and equipment etc., In a reduced form the Indian textile industry to become internationally competitive, action on three fronts is imperative—larger scale of production, greater capitalization and technology up-gradation. Wadje paper gives a SWOT analysis of Maharashtra textile industry which in it self is informative Wadjes papers underlines need for attracting foreign capital by proper display of potential, proper organizational development involving export-import market, continous product development and total quality management. He has rightly pointed out that textile industry requires continuous power supply for being efficient and for using full capacity.

Dr. R.Y. Mahore in his paper implications of TRIPS with special reference to higher education in India gives a neat and simplified explanation of recent development in the field of GATS. He explains different concepts of education as service and how it is connected with international trade. He also explains 5 categories of education services he explains the principle of progressive liberalization and its effects on education in developing countries. He has given a list of 9 points for serious discussion. He further explains the concept of cost recovery, student fee, need for student loan, as also pull factors, push factors and external factors which have caused emergence and rapid expansion of private higher education in India. This paper highlights emerging issues in the field of higher education in India. Some of the issues relate to commercial presence of private foreign educational institutions, pricing of education, transition of education as right to education as privilege and expanding inequities in the field of higher education in India. Against this background Mahore mentions that for some time more higher education must continue to be in the public sector for which proper, adequate financing needs to be mobilized by resort to novel methods of collecting revenue from the people.

After elaborate comments and observations by participants of seminar it was realized that infrastructure development and access must continue to be public utilities with objective economic pricing and targeted subsidization. It was fully realized that with proper scaling up, increasing capitalization and technology upgradation, Indian textile industry, more so Maharashtra textile industry has great potential for exports in various parts of the world. So for as higher education is concerned withdrawal by the state is totally disliked industry has great potential for exports in various parts of the world. So for as higher education is concerned withdrawal by the state is totally disliked and there is a general feeling that the government must continue to play a positive, substantial role in the formation, development and sustenance of higher education if socio-economically handicapped large majority of Indian population is to be given proper access to higher education in India, particularly in the field of technical, medical, managerial, financial, and research sectors of economic activity.

The papers by Dr. Basavraj, Dr. Mahore and Prof. Wadje were rightly appreciated by the participants for upto date references, rich data and posing of a vitally important social issues.

11

ECONOMIC REFORMS AND REGIONAL DISPARITIES IN INDIA

R.P. Kurulkar

INTRODUCTION

The problem of regional disparities in India has been in existence since the First Five Year Plan, which commenced in 1951. Reducing inter-state disparities in development has been one of the major objectives of our Five Year Plans. The latest Ninth and Tenth Plans have also made reference to reducing regional of inter-state disparities in India.

But, since 1991, India has adopted what is known as New Economic Policy, and, accordingly, have initiated several economic reforms in different sectors of the Indian economy. Those are mainly, Structural Adjustment Programmes, etc. Prior to 1991, India's economy was mostly a protected one and public sector dominated economy. It was getting stagnated and lacked efficiency, productivity and a reasonable growth rate. But since 1991, the Indian economy is being progressively integrated with the World Economy, through various policy measure like, liberalization (reducing high tariff walls), privatization (disinvestment policy), and opening the economy to private and foreign investors (portfolio investments and Foreign Direct Investments). The licence-permit raj has now come to an end, as industrial location policy has been abolished. Secondly, as India has become one of the founder members of World Trade Organization since 1995, it has become obligatory for India to follow various agreements relating to tariff rates, opening agriculture and service sectors to foreigners, etc. Shortly, India has joined now the Global Economy, or the Global market.

OBJECTIVE

This paper has the following major objectives:

(a) What has been the impact of various economic reforms initiated by the Govt. on 15 major states of the Indian Union, since 1991 for this purpose, the reference period has been divided into two parts.

  (i) The period between 1981 and 1991, is considered as pre-reform period, and,

  (ii) The period between 1991 and 2000, is considered as post-reform period.

(b) In section II, the objective is to identify the "most backward and poorest" districts in India. This may be considered as "Intra-State or Inter district" disparities in development. The basis of the discussion in this section is the recent "Sarma Committee Report of 1997.

(c) In Section III, the objective is to suggest various policy measures to reduce inter-district regional disparities in the country over the next 10 years.

An agenda for various economic reforms for the States in suggested with a view to ameliorate the deteriorating economic conditions of people residing in "most backward and poorest districts" in the country.

SECTION - I

IMPACT OF ECONOMIC REFORMS ON 15 MAJOR STATES OF THE INDIAN UNION

In this section, we propose to briefly examine the impact of various economic reforms mentioned earlier on the 15 major states of the Indian Union. For this purpose, we have compared the position of these states as it existed during the period 1981 to 1991. This may be termed as the pre-reform period; and the economic condition obtaining during the post-reform period, i.e., 1991 to 2000.

Impact on per capita Net State Domestic Product of States

Shows data relating to the per capita income of the 15 major states in India, for the year 1981 and 1991 (pre-reform period) and 1999–2000 (post reform period). For comparison, we have show State Relative Index for each state with All India per capita income as the base or 100.

(i) In 1981, the All India per capita income was Rs. 1741, and only six states had per capita income above this National average. These states were Punjab, Maharashtra, Harayana, Gujarat, West Bengal and Kerala. The remaining 9 states had per capita income below the National average. Bihar, Assam, Orissa, Uttar Pradesh and Rajasthan were at the bottom.

In 1991, the All India per capita income was found to be Rs. 5365; the number of states above this National average was 5; West Bengal and Kerala slipping below the National average, while Tamilnadu going above the National average.

In 2000, which is the post reform period, the All India per capita income was observed to be Rs. 15562; the number of states with per capita income above the National average increased from 5 in 1991 to 8 in 2000. West Bengal, Kerala and Karnataka joining the states with per capita incomes above the National average.

Punjab, Maharashtra, Haryana and Gujarat have almost maintained their relative position in terms of State Relative Index. On the other hand, Bihar, Orissa, Uttar Pradesh and Madhya Pradesh have shown a constantly deteriorating economic conditions reflected in their declining state relative indices, through 1981 to 2000. The state of Bihar, which is considered a problem state nowadays, has been at the bottom of the table during 1981, 1991 and 2000. Let us draw some major conclusions from this Table 1, relating to inter-state disparities in development.

(ii) The ratio between the lowest and highest per capita incomes of the States has increased from 2.57 in 1981 to 2.76 in 1991, and to 3.70 in the year 2000. This indicates a widening gap between least developed and most developed state in India, during the post reform period.

(iii) The standard deviation of per capita state incomes, has shown as increasing trend; the standard deviation which was 459.10 in 1981, increased to 1508.9 in 1991, and to 5196.3 in 2000.

(iv) The coefficient of variation of state per capita incomes also supports the conclusions that inter-state regional disparities have sharply increased during the post-reform period. The coefficient of variation of per capita income, which was 26.37% in 1981, increased to 28.12% in 1991 (pre-reform period), while it increased to 33.39% in 2000 (post-reform period).

Hence, we may draw one important conclusion based on the above mentioned statistical results that, during the post-reform period, the rich states have become richer while the poor states have become poorer.

Impact on Poverty

Let us now Study the impact of economic reforms on the proportion of population below the poverty line in 15 major states, for the year, 1987–88, 1993–94 and 1999–2000. The relevant data are indicated in Table 2. At the All India level, the proportion of population below the poverty line, in 1987–88, was 38.9%; but in 1993–94, and 1999–2000, it declined to 36.9% and 26.1% respectively. (post-reform period). This should be considered as a very positive impact of reforms on reducing poverty levels.

But at the state-level, the impact of reforms is of varying degrees during the reference period. The proportion of population below the poverty line was very high in backward states in 1987–88; i.e. Orissa 55.6%; Bihar 52.1% Madhya Pradesh 43.1% Uttar Pradesh 41.5% etc., while on the other hand, the proportion of population below the poverty line was relatively very low in advanced states, like, Punjab 13.2% Haryana 16.6%, Gujrat 31.5%, Kerala 31.8% etc.

Table 2
Impact of Economic Reforms on Poverty and Employment in India: (Selected Major States)

Sl. No.	State	Poverty Ratio (% of Population)			Poverty (Reduction %)		Growth of Empoloyment			
		87–88	93–94	99–00	87–88 93–94	93–94 99–2000	1983 Urban	1993–94 Rural	1993–94 to 1999–2000 Urban	Rural
1.	Punajb	13.2	11.8	6.2	1.4	5.6	2.1	0.6	2.6	2.5
2.	Maharashtra	40.4	36.9	25.0	3.5	11.9	2.9	1.9	1.9	0.6
3.	Haryana	16.6	25.1	8.7	8.5	16.4	3.8	2.8	0.8	0.5
4.	Gujrat	31.5	24.2	14.1	7.3	6.8	3.3	1.7	2.3	2.0
5.	West Bengal	44.7	35.7	27.0	9.0	8.7	2.0	1.5	0.8	1.2
6.	Kerala	31.8	25.4	12.7	6.4	6.3	4.4	0.1	3.2	0.9
7.	Tamilnadu	43.4	35.0	21.1	8.4	13.9	2.4	1.6	1.6	0.4
8.	Karnataka	37.5	33.2	20.0	4.2	13.2	2.2	2.3	2.8	1.2
9.	Madhya Pradesh	43.1	42.5	37.4	0.6	9.7	3.3	1.9	3.3	1.4
10.	Andhra Pradesh	25.9	22.2	15.8	3.7	12.1	3.7	2.0	2.2	0.8
11.	Rajasthan	35.2	27.4	15.3	7.5	7.8	2.8	2.5	2.4	1.4
12.	Uttar Pradesh	41.5	40.9	31.2	0.6	9.7	2.9	1.8	3.3	1.4
13.	Orissa	55.6	48.6	47.0	7.0	1.5	3.3	2.0	3.4	1.0
14.	Assam	36.2	40.9	36.1	4.7	4.8	1.0	1.7	2.7	2.4
15.	Bihar	52.1	55.0	42.6	2.9	12.4	0.9	0.9	3.6	2.3
All India		38.9	36.9	26.1	2.0	9.9	2.9	1.8	2.4	1.3

Source: Indian Economy: Rudder Dutt & Sundaram p.370 S.Chand.
* Statistical outline of India: 2002–03, Tafa Services Limited, p. 155.

In the year 1993–94, which was the initial phase of the economic reforms, the proportion of population below the poverty line has declined in 12 states; while it has increased in three states, viz. Haryana, Assam and Bihar.

Between 1993–94 and 1999–2000, there was further reduction in poverty in all the 15 states, in varying degrees. But in backward states the reduction in poverty was marginal, while in advanced states it was quite substantial, e.g. Haryana, Maharashtra, Punjab, Karnataka, Tamilnadu, etc. Therefore, the proportion of poverty in poorer states is very high even in 2000. i.e. Orissa 47.1%, Madhya Pradesh 37.4%, Assam 361.%, Uttar Pradesh 31.2% etc.

From the above analysis we may draw one important conclusion that during the post-reforms period, the poverty ratios of all the 15 major states have declined to a considerable extent. At the all India level, the poverty ratio has sharply declined from 36.9% in 1993–94 to 26.1% in 1999–2000, or by about 10%.

Impact on Growth of Employment

Poverty and unemployment are two sides of the same coin; this is especially true of the people without any assets. Table 2 also shows the growth of employment during the pre (1983) and post reform periods (1999–2000). At the All India level, the growth rate of urban employment has declined from 2.9% in (1983–93) to 2.4% in (1993–94–1999–2000). Similarly, the growth rate of rural employment has also fallen from 1.8% in 1983, to 1.3% in 1999–2000. This situation has led to rising levels of unemployment, mainly due to various economic reforms. This is perhaps the most serious and negative impact of economic reforms in India. We have a high growth rate of the GDP accompanied by declining growth rate of employment, in other words we have "jobless growth".

At the state level, the growth rate of urban employment has declined in the following states during the reference period, viz. Maharashtra, Haryana, Gujrat, West Bengal, Kerala, Andhra Pradesh and Rajasthan (mostly advanced states). While the urban employment growth rates have improved in the following States, viz. Punjab, Tamilnadu, Uttar Pradesh, Orissa, Assam & Bihar (mostly backward states).

Similarly, the rates of growth of rural employment have declined in the following states, as an impact of economic reforms, during the same period. viz. Maharashtra, Haryana, West Bengal, Kerala, Tamilnadu, Karnataka, Madhya Pradesh, Andhra Pradesh, Rajasthan and Uttar Pradesh. On the other hand there are few states where growth rate of rural employment has improved, viz. Punjab, Gujarat, Kerala, Assam and Bihar.

The NSS Survey 55th Round (1999–2000) indicates rising levels of unemployment rates (CDS) in Indian States. For example, the unemployment rate was highest (20.97%) in Kerala; 14.99% in West Bengal, 11.78% in Tamilnadu, and minimum at 2.96% in Himachal Pradesh. At all India level, the unemployment was 7.32%.

Another important change which has taken place in the labour market during the post-reform period relates to the changing proportion of organized and unorganized labour markets. Earlier, about 10% of the labour was working in the organized labour market (of about 397 million), now the percentage has come down to only 7%; the army of the unorganised labour has increased to 93%, during post reform period.

Impact on Human Development

Ever since the publication of the Human Development Report-1990, under the guidance of Mahbubul Haq, the measurement of welfare of the common masses has shifted from per capita income to Human Development index. It is now agreed that the latter is more appropriate measure of welfare than the former. The UNDP Human Development Report (1997). Describes the concept of Human Development in the following words:

> "The process of widening propels choices and the level of well being they achieve are at the core of the notion of human development. Such theories are neither finite nor static. But regardless of the level of development, the essential choices for the people are to lead a long and healthy life, to acquire knowledge and to have access to the resources needed for a decent standard of life. Other choices highly valued by many people, range from political, economic and social freedom to opportunities for being creative and productive and enjoying self-respect and guaranteed human rights" (UNDP Human Development Report (1997).

Human Development Index (HDI) measures the average achievements in three basic dimensions of human development.

(i) A long and healthy life as measured by life expectancy at birth or longevity.

(ii) Knowledge as measured by adult literacy rate (with two-third weight) and combined primary, secondary and territory gross enrolment ratio (with one-third weightage).

(iii) A decent standard of living as measured by GDP per capita (PPPUS dollars).

In Table 3, we have shown Human Development Indices, for 15 major states of the Indian Union, for the year, 1981, 1991, and 2001. In 1981, the All India value of HDI, was found to be 0.302, indicating a very low level of human development. But among the States, Kerala occupied top position with the HDI value of 0.500. There are 8 state in the table, which have HDI value above the all India average. All these states are "developed states". On the the other hand the remaining 7 states have lower HDI values than the National average.

In the year 1991, the All India HDI value has improved to 0.381, indicating improvement in literacy rate, schooling years and longevity and per capita income. Among the states, Kerala States has again topped the list with HDI value of 0.591. Other developed States have also improved their position. But the backward states have made little progress.

In the year 2001, which is a post-reform year, the All India HDI value has increased to 0.472. Among the States Kerala is again at the top. Punjab, Maharashtra, Tamilnadu and Haryana have made considerable progress, with HDI values above 0.5. Most of the BIMARU States are at the bottom of the table i.e. Bihar Madhya Pradesh, Rajasthen and Uttar Pradesh.

It is interesting note that although Kerala occupies top position in Human Development, still it ranks 9th in terms of per capita income. Similarly, Maharashtra tops the list in per capita income (1997–98) even then it ranks 4th in Human Development.

We may conclude from this analysis that, the backward states have not only low per capita income but they have a very low level of human development, over the years.

Table 3

Human Development Index for India, (For Selected Major States) 1981, 1991, 2001

Sl. No.	State	*HDI-Value* 1981	*HDI-Rank* 1981	*HDI Value* 1991	*HDI Rank* 1991	*HDI Value* 2001	*HDI Rank* 2001	*Per Capita (Rs.) NSDP (1997–98)*	*Rank*
1.	Punajb	0.500	1	0.591	1	0.638	1	2490	9
2.	Maharashtra	0.411	2	0.475	2	0.537	2	4389	2
3.	Haryana	0.363	3	0.452	3	0.523	4	5032	1
4.	Gujrat	0.360	4	0.431	4	0.479	6	3918	4
5.	West Bengal	0.360	5	0.443	5	0.509	5	4025	3
6.	Kerala	0.346	6	0.412	6	0.478	7	2866	7
7.	Tamilnadu	0.343	7	0.466	7	0.531	3	3141	5
8.	Karnataka	0.305	8	0.404	8	0.472	8	2977	6
9.	Madhya Pradesh	0.298	9	0.377	9	0.416	10	2550	8
10.	Andhra Pradesh	0.272	10	0.348	10	0.486	14	1675	13
11.	Rajasthan	0.267	11	0.345	11	0.404	11	1666	14
12.	Uttar Pradesh	0.256	12	0.347	12	0.424	9	2226	10
13.	Orissa	0.255	13	0.314	13	0.388	13	1725	12
14.	Assam	0.245	14	0.328	14	0.394	12	1922	11
15.	Bihar	0.237	15	0.308	15	0.367	15	1126	15
All India		0.302	–	0.381	–	0.472	–	2840	–

Source: Planning Commission (2002), National Human Development Report 2001.

Impact of Economic Reforms on Annual Average Growth Rates of Net State Domestic Products of Major States

Table 4 shows the annual average growth rates of the net State Domestic Products of the 15 major States for the period 1981–91 (pre-reform period) and 1990–91 to 1997–98 (or post-reform period). It will be observed from this table that the growth rates of forward states taken together, were 5.2% and 6.3% during the pre-reform post-reform period respectively. During the post-reform period, some of the forward State have achieved impressive growth rates, e.g. Gujrat, 7.9% Maharashtra 6.7% Karnataka 6.0%, Andhra Pradesh 6.3% etc. On the other hand, the Backward States have indicated a very poor performance, during the post-reform period, e.g. Bihar, 0.6%, Uttar Pradesh, 2.6%, Assam 3.3%, Rajasthan 4.0% etc. The growth rate achieved by all the Backward States together was found to be only 3.0%, during the post-reform period.

Table 4

Average Annual Growth Rates of Forward and Backward States (%)

Sl. No.	*State*	*1980–81 to 1990–91*	*1990–91 to 1997–98*
	Forward States	5.2	6.3
1	Punjab	5.3	4.4
2.	Maharashtra	6.0	6.7
3.	Haryana	6.5	4.0
4.	Gujrat	5.2	7.9
5.	West Bengal	4.2	6.7
6.	Kerala	3.2	5.8
7.	Tamilnadu	5.6	5.6
8.	Karnatka	5.0	6.0
9.	Andhra Pradesh	4.8	6.3
	Backward States	4.9	3.0
10.	Madhya Pradesh	4.7	4.1
11.	Rajasthan	7.4	4.0
12.	Uttar Pradesh	5.0	2.6
13.	Orissa	7.4	4.0
14	Assam	2.3	4.7
15	Bihar	4.9	0.6
	All India	5.6	5.4

Source: Handbook of Statistics on Indian Economy (1999) RBI.

1. There are two major reasons which have retarded the growth rates of Backward States during the post reform period. First, due to abolition of location policy, de-licensing of industrial policy, and opening the economy to Foreign Direct Investment (FDI), the already developed states like Maharashtra, Gujarat, Tamilnadu, Karnataka, Punjab, etc. could attract large proportion of FDI in their states. They could attract FDI funds mainly because of relatively better infrastructure (roads, power, rail, air) and availability of skilled manpower. On the other hand, most backward states like Bihar, UP, Orissa, M.P. lacked these facilities, and, hence they could not attract FDI funds to their states. This may be considered as major reason for rising disparities in development between rich and poor states.
2. Secondly, the public investment in agriculture in these states had declined to a considerable extent during the post-reform period. As these backward States are highly dependent on agriculture for their livelihood, reduction of public investment has badly affected the growth rates of these States.
3. At all India level, however, we have been able to cross the barrier of the "Hindu Rate of Growth" (3.5%), during the post reform period. (i.e. 6.5% to 7%). This is most positive impact of economic reforms during the post reform period.

SECTION-II

INDIA'S 100 MOST BACKWARD DISTRICTS

In section-I, we have discussed the impact of economic reform, on 15 major states of the Indian economy and have come to conclusion that, during the post-reform period, (1991–2000), the inter-state disparities have sharply increased. The backward states have shown a very low growth rate of the State Domestic Product, high poverty ratios, and very low human development values.

In this section II, we shall specifically identify the number of "poorest" or "most-backward districts" in the country. For this purpose we shall briefly discuss the findings of the Sarma Committee Report (1997), which are quite relevant today. The Sarma

Committee identified India's "100 poorest and most backward districts" in the country by adopting certain socio-economic criteria, which are briefly stated below:

(a) Indicators of Deprivation, like poverty ratio, education and health, (3)

(b) Indicators of social infrastructure. (5)

(c) Indicators of economic infrastructure. (8)

On the basis of these 16 indicators, the Committee has identified 100 poorest districts in the country's the State-wise position is as follows:

> (1) Bihar 38 districts (2) Madhya Pradesh—19 districts (3) Uttar Pradesh—17 districts (4) Maharashtra 10 districts. (5) Orissa—4 districts (6) West Bangal—4 districts (7) Rasjasthan—2 districts. (8) Sikkim—2 districts (9) Karnataka—1 districts (10) Haryana—1districts (11) Himchal Pradesh—1district (12 Dadra-Nagar-Haveli—1district = Total 100.

These 100 most backward districts are located in 12 states of the Indian Union. Of these 100 majority (80) of them are located in the so-called BIMARU States. It is interesting to note that, an economically advanced state like Maharashtra has 10 poorest districts (or 10% of the total). Similarly, some of the advanced states like West Bengal, Karnataka, Harayana also have backward districts identified by the Committee.

Therefore, it may be concluded from the above data, that, backward districts are mostly located in already identified backward states; however, even advanced states have pockets of backward areas or district. In the light of this conclusion, let us now examine as to what kind of economic policies need to be implemented in these most backward districts, which form sizable part of the population of India.

SECTION-III

AGENDA FOR REFORMS AT THE STATE LEVEL

The agenda for reforms at the State level should aim at increasing the rate of growth and level of human development in backward states. During the next decade the reforms to which the states need to give priority are*.

(i) Reduction in subsidies related to consumption of power by the agriculture and domestic sectors, along with restructuring of the State Electricity Boards, to make them more autonomous and efficient.

(ii) Improvement in the quality of roads and the extension of the road network.

(iii) Removal of hindrances to the free movement of goods to the maximum possible extent.

(iv) Closing down or sale of loss making public enterprises.

(v) Reforms of the tax structure, particularly the introduction of the State value Added Tax (VAT), and improvement of tax administration through computerization.

(vi) Adopting a planned approach to expenditure growth and achieving zero deficit on the revenue account within the next five years.

(vii) Higher outlays on primary and secondary education, health and family planning, with significant improvements in the standard of services.

The above mentioned agenda for state-level reforms are of a general nature. This agenda may differ from state to state considering their level of development. As our objective is to improve the economic conditions in 150 most backward districts in the country our priority may be different to achieve these objectives. We shall discuss these issues in the next section.

ACTION PLAN FOR DEVELOPMENT OF 100 MOST BACKWARD DISTRICTS IN THE COUNTRY: AN AGENDA FOR REFORMS AT STATE LEVEL

(i) In this section an attempt is made to examine the role of the State Govt. to initiate an action Plan for the economic development of the poorest people in the country. Unless some

---

* R.J. Chelliah: Reducing Poverty through State-level Reforms; (2004) Economic Reforms in South Asia, p. 34.

special efforts are made in this direction, the social and economic upliftment of their vast areas and people residing there is not possible. Fortunately, the United Progressive Alliance Govt. has taken a positive stand to initiate various developmental programmes in these 100 (or 150) most backward districts in the country. The Common Minimum Programme (CMP), has mentioned various policy measures to reduce regional imbalance in the country. All these policy measures need to be implemented at the State level during the next 5 years. We shall discuss some of the important policy measures which could be implemented by both Central and State Governments with a view to ameliorate the economic conditions of the poorest people in the country.

(ii) The Nature of the Problem: In the first section of this paper, we have examined in detail the present economic and social condition of backward areas, with reference to per capita income, Human Development status, rate of growth of the State Domestic product, rate of unemployment. etc. In the light of these variables, we may note that problems of all these backward areas very common in all states. Specifically they may be stated as follows:

(a) Heavy dependence of population on agriculture and allied activities.

(b) Large proportion of landless and agricultural labour.

(c) Large proportion of marginal and small farmers.

(d) Very low proportion of irrigation facilities.

(e) Very low productivity of crops per hectare.

(f) Large proportion of population below the poverty line.

(g) Low Human Development Index, i.e.

Indicating low literacy rates, especially, low female literacy rate, lower proportion of population having access to safe drinking water, health services, and sanitation facilities.

(h) high drops out rates among primary and secondary education mainly due to poverty.

(iii) Recently, the United Progressive Alliance (UPA) Government, under its common Minimum Programme (CMP), has introduced a bill, "the National Rural Employment Act 2004" in Parliament. The main features of the bill are (1) one adult person in a family (below the poverty line) is guaranteed employment for 100 days in a year. (2) If the Govt. fails to offer employment the job seeker is to be paid an unemployment allowance. (3) Wages are to be paid partly in cash and partly in kind (under food for work programme) at minimum wage rates. (4) The cost of the scheme is estimated between Rs. 44100 and Rs. 53100 Crores by various economists. We suggest that the coverage of the scheme should be extended to all able bodied persons in poor families and should be operated through out the year. According to T.S. Papola the actual cost of the scheme may be much smaller than the estimated by some economists.

(iv) According to the budget speech of the Finance Minister on 28th Feb. 2005 the Govt. has created the Backward States Grant Fund by providing Rs. 5000 crores in the annual budget. This is the most welcome proposal by the Finance Minister to provide financial help to the 150 most backward districts in the country.

THE ROLE OF THE CENTRAL PLANNING COMMISSION

(i) We suggest that the Central Planning Commission should take upon itself the responsibility of the development of all identified 150 most backward districts in the country. The Planning Commission should make available necessary funds through various types of grants to these backward areas.

A special component or sub-plan approach should be adopted at the National and State level. This approach, it appears, is supported by eminent economist, R.J. Chelliah, in the following remarks,: "The Centre will have to conceive and implement special plans to supplement the efforts of the poorest states to accelerate their growth and to promote faster human development." About the changing role of the Planning Commission, he says, "The Planning Commission should rather concentrate on helping to bring about the transformation of the backward states".

Another eminent economist, Alakh N.Sharma, has also expressed similar views regarding Central help to backward areas. He says, "The Central Government has to help them in this regard not only in terms of larger budgetary allocations but more by assisting them in attracting larger domestic and international investments. The direct role of the Central Govt. would be particularly crucial in providing available resources for infra-structural development."

The Common Minimum Programme (CMP) has also taken a serious note of the widening regional disparities in the country. It says: "The UPA Government is committed to redressing growing regional imbalances both among the States as well as within states, through fiscal, administrative, investment and other means... the UPA Government will consider the creation of a Backward States Grant Fund, that will be used to create productive assets in these states"

(ii) Projects should be designed as area development projects with location specific sub-projects for administrative sub-units like talukas/blocks etc. or specific problems like potential areas like command area development or "drought-prone area development," etc. The grants given by the Planning Commission, should be conditional and project/programme specific. These funds should not be divertible by the State Govt. to any other purpose or to any other region/district of the State. There should be strict monitoring over the progress and achievements of the programmes, by the Planning Commission.

(iv) The Central Govt. should impress upon the State Govt. to allocate at least 10% of their Annual Plan funds, as "Special Funds" for the faster development of backward districts/regions in their states. It is our experience that developed regions in various states, have been appropriating major portion of the plan funds to their regions; this has led to rising levels of inter-district disparities in States like U.P., Bihar, M.P., Andhra Pradesh, Maharashtra, etc. therefore, the above mentioned state level financial reforms are urgently required.

(v) All State Finance Commissions in India, have not been giving any special weightage to Panchayat Raj Institutions and Municipalities in backward districts, regarding allocation of non-plan funds. Such a weightage should be included in their terms of reference.

(vi) The State Govt. in their Annual Plans, should allocate some proportion of plan funds, to the "District Planning Committees" (DPC), on the basis of the Human Development Index of the district. This kind of reform in the financial sector of the State Govt. will ensure adequate-funds to relatively backward districts in human development. (i.e. literacy, primary education, health services, etc.)

(vii) The States in which there are large no. of backward states, like Bihar, Uttar Pradesh, Madhya Pradesh, etc. the Govt. may establish Regional Development Boards, for these backward districts. These Boards may keep a close watch on the proper allocation of plan funds, or other grants received for development of these districts. These Boards may prepare "Regional Plans" for these districts, under the guidance of the State Planning Boards/Departments. Such Boards are in operation in Maharashtra since the last 10 years. They are specifically created by the President of India Under Article 371 (2) of the Constitution. The objectives and functions of these Boards may be state specific to suit the purpose. These Boards are considered as a mechanism to remove relative economic backwardness in Maharashtra. Such Boards could be replicated, for example, for Eastern Uttar Pradesh, Bihar, Madhya Pradesh, Andhra Pradesh etc. Where large chunk of areas are extremely backward.

All these state-level reforms need to be addressed urgently.

REFERENCES

Economics Survey, (2001–02), Govt. of India, Ministry of Finance, (Economic Division).

Statistical out-line of India, (2002–03), Tata-Servcies, Ltd. Mumbai.

National Human Development Report (2001), Planning Commission, Govt. of India.

Indian Economy, Rudder Dutta & Sundaram, S. Chand, New Delhi.

National Common Minimum Programme of the Govt. of India. May 2004.

Kurulkar, R.P. and Varudkar, S.L. (2001), Action Plan for Backward District Development, Unpublished paper presented at the National Conference on "Backward Districts Development", held at Bangalore on 13th, 14th July.

Chelliah, R.J. (2004), "Reducing Poverty through State-level Reforms" in Economic Liberalization in South Asia.

Sharma, Alakh W. and Lakdawala, D.T. (2004), Globalization, Labour Markets and Poverty: Emerging Perspectives in India, Memorial Lecture, delivered at 87th Conference of the Indian Economic Association held at Banaras, Hindu University, Dec. 21.

Papola, T.S. (2005), A Universal Programme is Feasible: Economic and Political Weekly, Feb. 12, 2005 Mumbai.

Human Development Reports, 1997, 98, 99, 2000. UNDP.

Sarma Committee Report for Identification of 100 Most Backward and Poorest Districts in the Country. Govt of India, 1997.

12

AGENDA OF ECONOMIC REFORMS FOR THE STATES IN INDIA

V.S. Kulkarni

INTRODUCTION

The subject is very vast and the area required to be covered also is from the National Economy at one end and the rural Micro Economy at the other end. The State subject fall in between. I have here tried to knot all the ties together in the economic scenario specially in connection with the Service Sector Agenda & that to Banks & Finance.

India is very vast country comprising of 28 States & 7 Union territories. These are also again full of diversities and the scale of progress can range from 100 to 0 depending upon the reach & political will. Even if we take the case of Maharashtra which comprises of Geographical Zones such as;

(a) Paschim Maharashtra

(b) Kokan

(c) Vidharbha

(d) Marathwada

The same is the case of other states. This makes the proposition very vast & compression will lead me to restrict myself to some confined areas.

Economic Reforms started in all the fields like Agriculture, Industry, Service Sector since 1990–91 in real sense. Prior to that the Agriculture reforms Kool Kayada etc started right since independence. The Industrial Reforms started in 1955–56. Banking which is the major key of Economic Reform goes way back to 1970 towards socialization and now it has taken the turn towards the consolidation, Mergers and Acquisition.

The co-operative movement cannot be ignored while talking about the reforms for the States. This has its routes in mainly the agriculture sector, rural/semi-urban centres.

I shall however keep myself confined to the service sector Agenda of Economic Reforms.

ECONOMIC REFORMS—CENTRAL GOVT/STATE GOVT: AN OVERVIEW

India's economic reforms have played a critical role in the performance of the economy since 1991. It is important to note that despite the slowdown in 1997–98, the average growth rate in the four years, 1994--45 to 1997–98 was 6.9 per cent, Significantly higher than the growth rate of 5.6 per cent achieved in the 1980s. Moreover, the growth in the 1980s was not sustainable without further reforms, as the lack of export dynamism contributed to a balance of payments crisis at the end of the decade. Two significant measures were taken by the NDA government in 1999 that indicated the Government of India's continued commitment to the economic reform process. These were: the passage of the Insurance Regulatory and Development Authority (IRDA) Act 1999 in parliament and a substantial increase in the administered prices of diesel; despite fierce opposition from several quarters, including a long drawn strike by truckers in October 1999. The passage of IRDA Act by the parliament was a major milestone in India's on-going economic liberalization process as it opened the way for the private sector in the insurance business, which had been a government monopoly for decades. The year 2003–04 witnessed consolidation of gains achieved in respect of finance of Central Govt. It also paved the way for the enactment of the Fiscal responsibility & Budget Management Act 2003 which will definitely lead towards better financial discipline.

It is heartening that the change over of the Govt has not only kept the pace of further liberalization but is committed for the over all sustained growth orientated economy. This has reflected in the several measures such as incremental FII investment in telecom, infrastructure, construction activity. The proposed policy of Banks Consolidation & Acquisition, Mergers & Amalgamations. Enhancing the voting rights beyond 10% in Banking to the acquire are the signs which would really excel the growth with stability.

As with the central government, the financial condition of the state governments in India has also been a cause for concern. Over the years, the consolidated financial position of the state governments has shown a marked deterioration in some of their major deficit indicators. One of the fundamental weaknesses of state government finances in India can be attributed to the increases in non-developmental expenditure, particularly the revenue component of the non-developmental expenditure, and interest payments as a proportion of revenue receipts. These problems have been greatly aggravated over the past few years for a variety of reasons. The resource constraints in state finances have been accentuated by a near stagnant tax-GDP ratio, a rising share of non-developmental outlay in the total expenditure, large volumes of hidden or implicit subsidies and increasing financial losses of state enterprises.

A growing pressure on state finances has also stemmed from the rising demand for public services. Furthermore, the fiscal situation in the states is likely to come under much greater pressure with the acceptance of the report of the Fifth Pay Commission by several state governments in India & populist measures such as free electricity & incremental state subsidies. The slow growth in revenue mobilization at the state level has posed serious difficulties for the state governments to meet their expenditures. Be that as it may, the critical problem in state finances is not only one of high levels of expenditure, but also one of increasing distortions in the pattern of expenditure.

In the final analysis, fiscal control will require an overhaul not just in budgetary patterns, but in the basic functioning of the public sector in the economy. For example, privatization is an important means to reduce the overhang of public debt. Similarly, privatization of infrastructure services is a key method to relieve the growing burden on state budgets, which are weighed down by losses of State Electricity Boards (SEBs) and other parastatal institutions.

Greater autonomy for local and state-level governments in infrastructure reforms and investment priorities will similarly allow the central government greater freedom in cutting back on transfer payments to the states, which will be in a better position to prioritize and economize on state spending.

A few of the Indian states have been more reform-oriented, such as Andhra Pradesh, Gujarat, Karnataka, Maharashtra, and Tamil Nadu, while states such as Haryana, Kerala, Orissa, Madhya Pradesh, Punjab, Rajasthan, and West Bengal have lagged in carrying out state-level reforms. Bihar and Uttar Pradesh are even further behind. States that move against the populist policies and set up regular markets for services, such as power and water, are going to be ahead of the rest in the game. They are likely to garner faster state-level economic growth and job creation, from both domestic and foreign investments.

Broadly speaking, there are currently rather significant differences in reform interest and economic performance between a large part of northern India and southern India. Karnataka, Tamil Nadu, and Andhra Pradesh are quite dynamic now in trying to improve the physical and legal infrastructure, in order to attract large-scale foreign investment. In the north especially in Bihar and Uttar Pradesh, one does not see the same kind of reform dynamism and the results are therefore poor in terms of economic growth. It is expected that these differences will be noticed politically sooner rather than later, as inequalities between states in their economic performance become glaring. The states that are ahead will be rewarded with better performance while the states that are behind will find that there is the demand to catch up with the states that are growing. This kind of inter-state competition will spur the overall reform process, as has the inter-regional competition in China.

There will be continued inflationary pressures in the ensuing years because of hardening of International oil prices & depreciating US dollar. The pressure on hardening of the interest rates shall also be very much there.

Early developments in 2004–05 present several continuing strengths in the economy though accompanied by some uncertainties. Industrial activity has gathered strength. The industrial climate reflects a revival of investment demand and building up of capacity. In particular, the capital goods and the intermediate goods sectors have recorded robust growth signifying the quickening of investment activity. This has been supported by improved corporate profitability, expansion in non-food credit and continuing optimism regarding production and export growth. On the other hand, production of consumer goods has slowed down considerably with the sustained growth in consumer durables providing a silver lining.

The net inflows in the form of FDI and ADRs/GDRs have gathered momentum. For the first quarter of 2004–05, the balance of payments recorded an overall surplus of US $ 7.5 billion. Reflecting these developments, the foreign exchange reserves crossed US $ 120 billion on July 2, 2004 before declining marginally to US $ 119.3 billion on August 13, 2004. Infact by Feb 2005, end the forex reserves has grown to the level of $132 billion which is the highest ever reserves and indicates the strength of economy. Over the rest of the year, the outlook for the balance of payments appears reasonably strong and resilient.

FINANCIAL SYSTEM: ROLE OF RESERVE BANK OF INDIA

The increasing market orientation of the financial system helps in improving allocative efficiency of resources. At the same time, however, it exposes both public sector and private sector financial intermediaries to various risks, necessitating prudential regulation and supervision. A key element of a market-oriented risk-based supervisory strategy is to develop sound corporate governance practices, which would minimise the need for process-focused supervision. The Reserve Bank, therefore, has been emphasising corporate governance and better risk assessment within banks and financial institutions, both public and private. The reforms required in the co-operative banking system, including the appropriate regulatory regime, is indeed welcome. The imperative of improving risk management systems must be seen as much from the angle of financial stability as from the process of economic development. Improved risk assessment systems are expected to enable banks to take greater exposures to sectors such as agriculture and small scale industries in which collateral valuations often pose difficulties.

This is all the more important as the pattern of credit demand has been changing in recent years. Demand for bank credit from large corporates has been declining because of financial restructuring, improvements in productivity, optimization of inventory cycles, better cash flow management, increased access to external commercial borrowings and improved internal generation of funds. With better risk assessment capabilities, banks should be able to shed their risk averse attitude and extend more finance to hitherto unbanked segments of agriculture, industry and services.

Management of the financial sector has been oriented towards gradual rebalancing between efficiency and stability and the changing shares of public and private ownership. Enhanced competition among diverse players has been encouraged. Regulation of urban co-operative banks is hampered by the system of dual control and speedy resolution of the issue is imperative to ensure the future health of the sector. Considerable improvements have taken place in prudential governance as also in moving away from administrative measures to market-orientation. Improvements in efficiency and stability are evident and there is merit in continuing with such rebalancing while refocusing on consolidation, governance and movement towards Basel II—*albeit* gradually, as in the past. Consolidation has started to encompass development finance institutions, public sector banks, private sector banks and non-bank financial companies. As the consolidation proceeds, it is necessary to design a road map so that over a period, there is a convergence between real sector reforms in India, a substantially liberalized capital account and an efficient but stable financial system, in particular the banking system, with an optimal diversity of players consistent with the growing size and complexity of the Indian economy. The consolidation mergers & acquisitions are therefore going to be the reality of the day in the near future for sustained growth & stability.

TECHNOLOGY IN BANKING

The technological infrastructure for the smooth and secure functioning of the payment system was strengthened with the implementation of Real Time Gross Settlement (RTGS) system, the Special Electronic Funds Transfer system and the Online Tax Accounting System. The Negotiated Dealing System (NDS)—Clearing Corporation of India Ltd. (CCIL) system enabled an improvement in LAF auctions by providing in a timely fashion, all the parameters such as issue duration, type of auctions and opening and closing time. The CCIL, which also offers a multilateral netting mechanism for inter-bank spot and forward dollar-rupee transactions, has provided time and cost benefits to banks. Introduction of exchange traded interest rate derivatives in the National Stock Exchange and allowing sale of Government security against existing purchase contract provided depth to the Government securities market which switched to the Delivery *versus* Payment (DVP II) mode with effect from April 2, 2004.

Technology has been the key driver of the revolutionary changes in the Indian financial sector with the increasing demand for inter connectivity, internet banking and Automated Teller Machine (ATM) centers. Net banking, phone banking, mobile banking, ATMs and bill payments are the new facilities that banks are using not only to attract customers but also to help them reduce their total operating costs. The introduction of computerization in the banking sector has led to considerable improvements in the functioning of clearing house mechanism, which facilitates the exchange of instruments, and processing of payment instructions at a central point among the participating banks. Clearing houses have gradually extended their range of activities to automate by electronic means the settlement of payment transactions.

NEW BANKING SCENARIO

Banking concept is under gone a major change in the last few years and it is widen as compared with the past concept of Banking. The Banks are offering the various other services under the one roof to its clients. It includes the services of Credit Cards, Debit Cards, Demate facility, Merchant Banking, Distribution of Insurance products etc.

PERFORMANCE OF BANKING SECTOR

While reviewing the performance we ought to take note at the outset of the varied challenges that the banks have faced in cleaning up and consolidating their operations in a new competitive environment in the 1990s. Apart from the need to improve the bottom line, to reduce non-performing assets and to observe the discipline of regulatory and prudential norms for capital adequacy, asset classification and income recognition, and provisioning, there has also occurred a sea-change in the role of banks as a result of competitive opportunities thrown up in para banking activities—merchant banking, housing finance, mutual funds, insurance and others, and above all, in the notion of universal banking and project finance. They have also spawned new financial products—market-based bonds as against traditional bank loans. These changes have been compounded by rapid technological advancement as well as structural changes in the economy. In a large measure, the evolution of banking after the 1990s reflects the banks' response to these organizational and market challenges faced by them.

The 1990s have also seen a more rapid expansion of high-street banking promoted by new private sector banks and foreign banks. As a result, even as the rural branches have stagnated or declined in number, the number of urban and metropolitan branches has galloped, from 17, 744 in March 1996 to 19, 597 in September 2003 —about 265 per year. There has also been some gentle rise in number of semi-urban branches. Rapid applications of new technology and significant structural changes in the Indian economy including the growth of the services sector and acceleration in urban orientation and sophistication in consumption, have provided an expanding space for high-street banking. Concurrently, the banks' reach for the rural population and the informal sectors seems to have suffered a setback—which, however, has turned out to be an unintended fallout of banking reforms. A glaring failure of public policy lies in the absence of any effective measure to fill the void so created in rural banking network. (Annexure-Appendix Table III 23).

RECEDING RURAL CREDIT-DEPOSIT RATIO

It is not only that rural branch network has stagnated but also that the relative sizes of rural deposits and credit have receded, and above all, the extent of credit deployed from out of deposits mobilized in rural areas has rapidly fallen. The shares of rural as well as semi-urban branches in aggregated deposits and credit have declined in the 1990s. The rural C-D ratio, which was over 65 per cent in the mid-1980s or 60 per cent in the early 1990s, has steadily slipped to around 42 per cent now. Similarly, the C-D ratios of semi-urban branches, which had remained around 49–50 per cent until the early 1990s, have declined rather precipitately and touched 35 per cent in September 2003. This is contrary to the 60 per cent C-D ratio prescribed by policy for rural and semi-urban branches. (Annexure-Appednix Table III 9).

Priority sector lending which forms the major position of Mass lending have two major categories, namely, agriculture (direct and indirect) and food processing, and small-scale industries. A distinct feature of recent banking trends has been the erosion in the share of bank credit for agriculture, food processing industries, small-scale industries and other informal sectors. The share of agriculture in total bank credit had reached 15.9 per cent and for small-scale industries 12.4 per cent in March 1990; these proportions fell to 11.3 per cent and 10.7 respectively, in March 1996. Thereafter, these proportions have experienced precipitate declines, with small-scale industries suffering the most during this period. While the medium and large-scale industry has sustained its share at about 38–39 per cent between 1996 and 2002, it is the 'services' sector that has obtained a larger share in this recent period, from about 40.7 per cent to 48.8 per cent. Interestingly, the decline in agricultural credit share has been particularly sharp amongst rural branches from 51.7 per cent in March 1996 to 44.7 per cent. On the other hand, as a result of many indirect lendings to "agriculture", the share of metropolitan branches has shot up from 9.5 per cent to 15.3 per cent. This is understandable as export credit extended by foreign banks in favour of food and agro-based processing sector has been included as part of "priority sectors" for achieving their target of 32 per cent. However, overall, the relative share of bank credit or food and agro-based industries has declined from 4.0 per cent to 3.2 per cent. (Annexure-Appendix Table III 24).

The Budget 2005–06, banks have been asked to increase the flow of credit by another 30 per cent in 2005–06 and also increase the number of farm borrowers by another 50 lacs. When the average rate of growth in agri-credit over the past decade has been 16 per cent, it will be difficult to sustain a 30 per cent disbursement target over the long term.

BANKS AND HOUSING FINANCE

Previously the finance to the housing sector was the monopoly of the financial institutions. But for the last few years Banks are playing a major role in financing the housing sector. For the purpose of achievement of the target of Priority Sector advances, banks were allowed to deploy funds under housing finance allocation in any of the following categories: (a) direct finance, (b) indirect finance, (c) investment in bonds of NHB/HUDCO or combination thereof, and (d) investment by banks in rated securities debt instruments issued by any Special Purpose Vehicle or entity representing housing loans granted by approved housing finance companies (under the supervision of NHB). The Central Govt's policy of offer the tax concessions for the repayment of principle up to Rs. 20000/- (previously) and interest payment of housing loan up to Rs. 1, 50,000/- have also helped for fast growth of housing finance. The Banks have increasingly taken interest in financing the Housing as one of the major activity. In the year 02–03 the housing loan portfolio was of Rs. 12308 crores & the same has jumped to over Rs. 52000 crores by March 04.

Two areas in which the scheduled commercial banks have done badly are: (i) lending for small size borrowers, and (ii) lending in favour of informal sectors. These in fact are responsible for the gross inequality in the distribution of banks credit sectorally. The small loans of up to Rs. 25,000 (or earlier up to Rs. 10,000) stands on a special footing. These are essentially informal sector loans and trends in them can offer significant commentaries on the attitudes of banks on such lendings. It is found that the number of such small borrowal accounts, which had reached the peak at 62.55 million in March 1992, has steadily dwindled thereafter and reached 37.22 million in March 2002, with the share of such accounts in total bank credit slipping from about 25 per cent to as low a figure as about 6 per cent. There has even occurred an absolute reduction in credit extended to such accounts from Rs. 41, 095 crore (12.5 per cent) in March 1998 to Rs 38, 501 crore (5.9 per cent) in March 2002. The combination of small loans and loans for unincorporated enterprises and individuals, broadly described as the "household" sector, has experienced a steady decline in its share in total credit in the 1990s.

Poverty alleviation and empowerment of the poor are better sustained in an environment of expanded credit delivery for micro-credit borrowers as much as for other small borrowers & hence the sustained credit flow with incremental coverage of areas & persons covered is the need for future economic growth.

There is another dimension to this spatial unequal distribution of bank credit. An extreme case is that of Maharashtra wherein the Mumbai metropolitan city alone accounts for 85.8 per cent of state's bank credit on utilization basis at the end of March 2002. Or the top five district account for 94.4 per cent of bank credit, leaving for the rest of 29 district just about 5.6 per cent of the state's total credit (Rs 11,501 crore); the latter contribute about 9.6 per cent (Rs. 21, 364 crore) of state's bank deposits.

Regional Rural Banks (RRBs) are another source of credit in rural areas. Several measures have been initiated to strengthen RRBs in the form of recapitalization of weak RRBs, relaxing lending to non-target group and deregulating deposit and lending rates.

DEVELOPMENTS IN CO-OPERATIVE BANKING

The co-operative banking system, with two broad segments of urban and rural co-operatives, forms an integral part of the Indian financial system. With a wide network and extensive coverage, these institutions have played an important developmental role in enlarging the ambit of institutional credit by way of inculcating banking habits among the poor and those in remote areas. In recent times, co-operative banks have tried to improve credit delivery through some financial innovations. (Annexure Appendix Table IV 1).

The Structure of co-operative banking[1] that has evolved over more than fifty years highlights the dual role of members as lenders and borrowers. The co-operative credit structure in the country can be divided into two broad segments: the urban co-operative banks and the rural co-operative credit institutions (Chart IV. 1) While the urban co-operative banking system has a single tier comprising

Chart IV. 1
Structure of Co-operative Credit Institutions

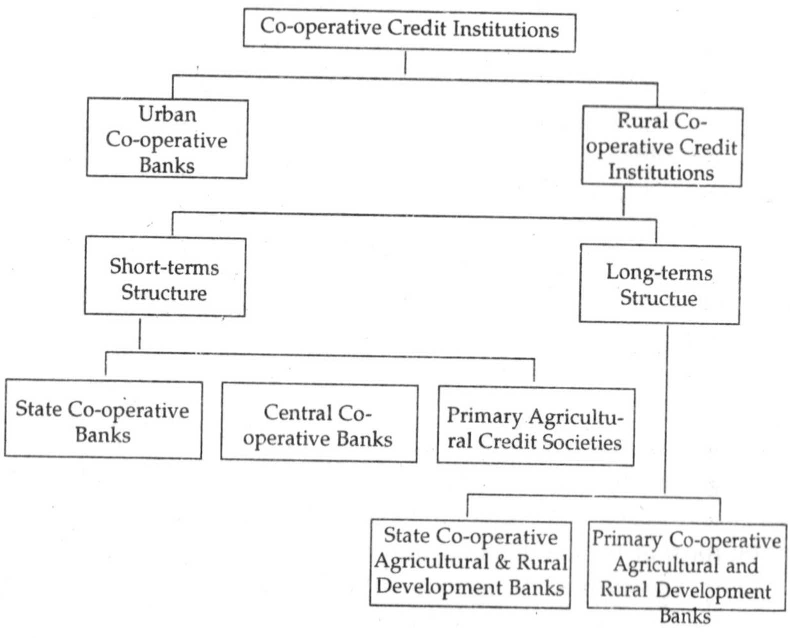

the primary Co-operative Banks (commonly known as urban co-operative banks-UCBs).

Under the Banking Regulation Act, 1949 only Urban Co-operative Banks (UCBs), State Co-operative Banks (StCBS) and Central Co-operative Banks (CCBS) are qualified to be called as banks in the co-operative sector.

Despite several years of operational experience, financial performance of a number of co-operative banks is still below their potential (Appendix Table IV. 1) The infusion of elements of good corporate governance, sound investment policy, appropriate internal control systems, better credit risk management, commitment to better customer service, and focus on newly-emerging business areas like micro finance, is expected to strengthen the co-operative banks. The Reserve Bank is in favour of a consultative approach to developing a regulatory framework and a revival plan in order to ensure a vibrant future for the co-operative sector, and thus encouraging systemic stability of the overall financial sector.

URBAN CO-OPERATIVE BANKS

Urban Co-operative Banks (UCBs) play an important role as financial intermediaries in urban and semi-urban areas catering to the needs of the non-agricultural sector, particularly small borrowers. In the context of the current economic scenario and problems faced by the co-operative banking sector, several initiatives were taken in consultation with the federations and associations of co-operative banks.

The number of UCBS increased to 2,105 including 179 banks under liquidation at end-June 2004 compared with 1,106 in 1966—the year in which the UCBs were brought under the purview of Banking Regulation Act 1949 (As Applicable to Co-operative Societies (AACS)). These include 80 salary earners banks, 112 Mahila banks and 25 SC/ST banks (Annexure Appendix Table IV 2).

RURAL CO-OPERATIVES

The short-term rural co-operative credit system in India comprising State co-operative banks (StCBs) at the apex (State) level, central co-operative banks (CCBs) at the intermediate (district) level and primary agricultural co-operative Societies (PACS) at the grassroot (village) level, is designed essentially to provide for short-term credit needs for production purposes. StCBs and CCBs have over the years grown substantially in terms of coverage and outreach, and at end-March 2003, their number stood at 30 and 367, respectively.

STATE CO-OPERATIVE BANKS

No StCB was included during 2003–04 in the Second schedule under Section 42 of the Reserve Banks of India Act, 1934. The total number of scheduled StCBs remained unchanged at 16 as on March 31, 2004.

KISAN CREDIT CARDS

In the Budget for 1998–99, an announcement was made for formulation of a model Scheme by NABARD for issue of Kisan Credit Cards (KCC) to farmers.

GIC has agreed that the crop loans disbursed for eligible crops under the Crop Insurance Scheme will be covered under the CCIS, now under Rashtriya Krishi Bima Yojana (RKBY).

The KCC Scheme is being implemented in all the States and Union Territories by all commercial banks, RRBs, state co-operative banks/central co-operative banks/PACS and scheduled primary co-operative banks. Up to March 31, 2004, these agencies had together issued 414 lakh cards indicating a wider acceptability of the KCC.

SELF HELP GROUPS

The SHG-bank linkage programme also has been positioned in the banking system as a commercial proposition, with advantages of lower transaction costs, near zero NPAs and generation of goodwill among the rural clientele for the bank branches leading to other quantifiable benefits in business expansion. All the 48 commercial banks and 196 RRBs now participate in the programme in addition to 316 out to total 368 CCBs. Formal Banking system has reached the doorstep of 116 lacs very poor households, providing micro-credit through 7.17 lacs SHGs.

ISSUES IN CO-OPERATIVE BANKING

Issues arising out of multiplicity of supervisory authorities continue to pose challenges in the co-operative banking sector. The Reserve Bank has repeatedly drawn the attention of the Government to the impact of multiple supervisory authorities on the performance of the co-operative banks. Cooperative banks are also subject to other difficulties ranging from members' apathy, imprudent investment decisions, low recovery rates, weak financial position and failure to modernise systems and procedures. Beside these, reconciling democratic character and financial discipline among these institutions is a challenge. Failure of a few co-operative banks has adverse implications for rest of the cooperative banks. A vision document is being evolved for the future role of Urban co-operative Banks (UCBs) which must ensure depositors' interests and avoid contagion while providing useful service to the local communities. The Reserve Bank would be encouraging growth of strong and viable entities through consolidation in the co-operative sector and sensitizing the State and Central Governments regarding the issues that arise in their jurisdiction.

The Reserve Bank has initiated several measure to mitigate the systemic implications of various risks prevailing in the co-operative sector. In its annual policy Statement 2004–05, the Reserve Bank announced that it would consider issuance of fresh licences only after a comprehensive policy on UCBs, including an appropriate legal and regulatory framework for the sector, is put in place. The Reserve Bank advised UCBs to classify an asset as doubtful with effect from March 31, 2005 if it remained in the sub-standard category for 12 months. Banks were however permitted to phase the consequent additional provisioning over a four-year period commencing from the year ending March 2005 with a minimum of 20 per cent each year.

CONSOLIDATION IN THE FINANCIAL SECTOR

The Indian banking sector is gradually heading towards consolidation of core competencies of different financial intermediaries and to universal banking, with banks being permitted to diversify into long-term finance and the DFIs into working capital. The universal banking may lead to greater economic efficiency in the form of lower cost, higher output and better products, but there is a need for caution in moving towards such a system by banks and FIs.

Consolidation in the financial sector has started encompassing development financial institutions, public sector banks and non-bank financing companies. The need is to design the consolidation process so as to achieve and harness convergence between the reforms undertaken in real sector, external sector and the financial sector. The Indian Bank's Association, the bankers' apex body, has recently set up a committee to look into the intricacies of mergers and acquisitions in the banking sector.

Increasing competition among banks, emanating not only from peers, but also from new entrants and other intermediaries, has been exerting pressure on bank spreads. The technology-intensive themselves as 'one-stop-shop' financial services and providing customers greater convenience and high quality services backed by appropriate investment in technology and other infrastructure. Therefore, the future profitability of banks would depend on their ability to generate greater non-interest income and control operating expenses. Blue-chip clients continue to have the option to raise low-cost funds directly from domestic and international markets. The reforms supported new environment is offering depositors and borrowers a wider range of opportunities to transact their business. Apart from the applicability of capital adequacy standards being in force, new methods of measuring market risk such as value-at risk and pre-commitment approaches are expected to provide a more standardized but tighter framework for the banking sector. Simultaneously, the banking industry is undergoing a change driven by technological advancements. Since retail customers are fast becoming more demanding, in the competitive environment, banks have to offer the value-added services. Harnessing technology to improve productivity so as to produce highly competitive types of banking and generating greater non-interest income by diversifying into non-fund based activities will be important features of the Indian banking of tomorrow.

CONCLUSION

In the earlier page I have taken a review of th national economic development so far the effects of liberalization and the Road Map or the canvass ahead of the Govt of India. The Role of Reserve Bank of India as the central financial authority also has been aptly dealt with. In any economic development the finance plays the catalytic role and hence the developments in this sector i.e. the Banks & financial Institutions which are the main pillars has also been reviewed. It will be observed that it is not single review but the contents which has the *"Blod Effect"* suggest the measures/ways & means and desired steps to be taken for marching ahead on the *"Economic Agenda of Sustanied Growth"*.

As regards the economic reforms agenda for the states in India many aspects have been dealt above while dealing with the financial reforms agenda. I have also enclosed a Road Map proposed by CII based on the Industrial Policy of Govt of Maharashtra 2001–2006. (Annexure CII Pens Refroms).

The said read map covers the areas "short and long term measures recommended include curbing of off-budget borrowings and guarantees, restructuring of the Maharashtra State Electricity Board, greater control over non-development expenditure, rationalizing of user charges, discontinuation of the cotton monopoly scheme, infrastructure development and privatization of ports, roads and power." As said by Mr. Trehan CII Chairman (Maharashtra).

The similar road map for the each state depending up on the financial stability space of growth required & the need to bring the last man/woman in the state into the growth process is needed.

The Document proposed by the task force appointed by Govt. of Maharashtra with M.N.Chaini, Deepak Satwalekar, Naseer Munjee, B.N.Makhija, Dr. Kirit Parikh and Ashoke Basak can also be taken into consideration as a road map for economic reforms agenda.

The Task Force which has come out with an excellent document, Vision 2005. Maharashtra Economic Development Council (MEDC) provided the needed data and technical support. The Task force has come out with an excellent document, "Vision 2005" giving a road map and the modus operandi to achieve the vision in a specific time frame. It is a blue print for prosperity through high growth rate. It aims at making every citizen in Maharashtra a 'Lakhpati" by 2010. The document is not a mere "wish list" but gives meaningful suggestions to achieve the goal. The task Force, without mincing words, has taken note of ground realities and exhorted the Government to be the "Facilitator" rather the "Doer". It strongly asserts Mrs Margaret Thather's off-quoted saying, "It is not Government's business to be in business". It has identified (a) IT (b) Bio-Tech (c) Entertainment (d) Exports as the growth drivers. The delineation of the issue of "Re-positioning Mumbai as a Mega Service Centre" is simply enchanting. The Task force has forcefully stressed the signficance of implementation aspect.

Tertiary sector which broadly corresponds to services sector needs special attention. Primary sector which refers to agriculture, mining and quarrying is virtually starved for bank finance.

A time bound action plan could be on the following lines:

1. Immediate identification of five or six banks in each of the Revenue Divisions.
2. These banks to be asked to float a subsidiary to provide 'investment finance' for large and mega projects.
3. The subsidiary to mobilize long-term resources through bonds to be guaranteed by the parent/sponsoring bank.
4. Rate of interest could be marginally higher than bank's long term deposit rates.
5. Banks should also set up Venture Capital funds (VCF) if required as their subsidiaries to cater to research-based ventures of technocrats with proven ability.
6. VCF resources could be locally raised with sponsor bank's guarantee. In addition, VCF could solicit funds from abroad towards equity.

7. VCF should be manned by young innovative experts who could be drawn from all available sources.
8. SSI units and small business have suffered during the major upheaval in the manufacturing sector in the last 5–6 years. Banks have the personnel, ability, knowledge and finance to help them. They need to be given autonomy. Vigilance angle should for sometime lie low.
9. Rural industrialisation can be a reality if banks are encouraged to function as the 'fulcrum' around which varied agro-processing activities could revolve.
10. Above-mentioned points could generate immense employment opportunities leading to social stability.

Agriculture needs a policy of plenty as well as a policy to manage plenty as the economic survey shows we have less wheat & rice today for every Indian than the 80's. The sessions attention needs to be given towards the population growth.

India is vastly dependent on imports for fuel, cooking oil & pulses. This needs to be improved a lot. The same is the case of infrastructure development & education.

Studies suggest that lenders in US capital markets believe that lending to states with fiscal constraints is less risky. We expect to find a similar experience in India if the states were to go to the market. Strict budget rules result in more controlled spending and less borrowing, reducing the cost of financing to states. Fiscal responsibility than mere legislation must be required of undeserving Indian states.

You will thus observe that there is no dearth of the financial institutions, corporates, social bodies which are ready and are actually supporting the Economic Agenda towards the Prosperity & Growth.

Last but not least I can say that lack of money is no obstacle, lack of suggestions also no obstacles but the lack of Ideas & Will towards implementation is the obstacle.

What needed is.....Action!!!

Appendix Table III.23
Region/State Unition Territory-wise Distribution of Commercial Bank Branches @

Sr. No.	Region/State/ Union Territory	Number of Branches as on June 30, end of June		Number of branches opened during				Average population (in '000) per bank branch as at the end of June	
		2002	2003	July 2001 to June 2002	of which: at un-banked centres	July 2002 to June 2003	of which: at un-banked centres	2002	2003
1	2	3	4	5	6	7	8	9	10
1.	Northern Region	10,709	10,809	148	1	120	6	12	13
	Chandigarh	175	182	6	0	7	0	5	5
	Delhi	1,478	1,489	39	0	26	0	10	11
	Haryana	1,557	1,580	25	0	23	0	13	13
	Himachal Pradesh	782	784	3	0	3	0	9	9
	Jammu & Kashmir	828	835	10	0	8	0	13	13
	Punjab	2,573	2.603	42	0	31	6	9	9
	Rajasthan	3,316	3,336	23	1	22	0	17	17
2.	North-Eastern Region	1,862	1,863	2	0	7	0	22	22
	Arunachal Pradesh	68	68	0	0	0	0	19	19
	Assam	1,212	1,212	1	0	6	0	22	22
	Manipur	77	77	0	0	0	0	35	36
	Meghalaya	180	180	1	0	0	0	14	15
	Mizoram	78	78	0	0	0	0	13	13
	Nagaland	70	70	0	0	0	0	26	26
	Tripura	177	178	0	0	1	0	23	23
3.	Eastern Region	11,736	11,748	42	1	29	0	19	19
	Andaman & Nicobar Islands	31	31	0	0	0	0	13	14
	Bihar	3,546	3,553	4	0	7	0	21	21
	Jharkhand	1,459	1,460	16	1	4	0	0**	0**

1	2	3	4	5	6	7	8	9	10
	Orissa	2.225	2,228	6	0	6	0	16	17
	Sikkim	48	48	1	0	0	0	12	13
	West Bengal	4,427	4,428	15	0	12	0	18	19
4.	Central Region	13,471	13,508	66	1	51	0	20	20
	Chattisgarh	1,035	1,037	5	0	4	0	0**	0**
	Madhya Pradesh	3,442	3,449	16	0	15	0	19	19
	Uttar Pradesh	8.148	8,169	37	1	24	0	20	20
	Uttaranchal	846	853	8	0	8	0	00**	0**
5.	Western Region	10,323	10,347	89	1	70	0	14	14
	Dadra & Nagar Haveli	11	12	0	0	1	0	18	17
	Daman & Diu	16	16	1	0	0	0	9	10
	Goa	328	329	5	0	1	0	5	5
	Gujarat	3,654	3,672	27	0	25	0	14	14
	Maharashtra	6,314	6,318	56	1	43	0	15	15
6.	Southern Region	18,158	18,239	201	8	141	3	13	13
	Andhra Pradesh	5,213	5,248	57	2	44	3	15	15
	Karnataka	4,770	4,797	49	2	44	0	11	11
	Kerala	3,346	3,374	54	4	32	0	10	10
	Lakshadweeap	9	9	0	0	0	0	8	9
	Pondicherry	82	84	1	0	2	0	14	14
	Tamil Nadu	4,738	4.727	40	0	19	0	13	13
	All India	66,259	66,514	548	12	418	9	16	16

@ Including the branches of non-scheduled commercial banks (Local Area Banks).

** As the population data of Jharkahand, Chhattisgarh and Uttaranchal are not separately avaialbel and included in Bihar. Madhya Pradesh and Uttar Pradesh States respectively, average population per bank branch for Bihar, Madhya Pradesh and Uttar Pradesh include the number of bank braches in Jharkhand, Chattisgarh and Uttarachal respectively.

Notes: 1. Average population per bank branch is based on estimated mid-year population of respective years received from the office of Registrar General and Census Commissioner, Government of India.

2. Bank branches excluse administrative offices.

3. Data for June 2002 are revised.

Appendix Table III.9
Region/State-wise Credit-Deposit Ratio and Investment plus Credit-Deposit Ratio of Scheduled Commercial Banks

(Per cent)

Sr. No.	Region/State/ Union Territory	Credit-Deposit Ratio							Investment plus Credit-Deposit Ratio @			
		2000		2001		2002	2003		2001		2002	
		As per Sanction	As per Utilisation	As per Sanction	As per Utilisation	As per Sanction	As per Utilisation	As per Sanction	As per Sanction	As per Utilisation	As per Sanction	As per Utilisation
1	2	3	4	5	6	7	8	9	10	11	12	13
1.	Northern Region	51.1	49.6	54.7	52.5	56.2	55.0	57.1	59.9	57.7	61.2	60.0
	Haryana	42.4	53.4	41.0	54.0	43.7	55.0	43.6	49.8	62.8	51.9	63.1
	Himachal Pradesh	23.8	26.8	21.3	25.7	23.4	32.5	24.7	35.5	39.9	36.3	45.4
	Jammu & Kashmir	33.5	30.9	34.5	33.5	36.8	40.9	37.9	42.7	41.8	46.0	50.1
	Punjab	39.4	40.9	41.1	42.3	41.8	43.9	41.6	47.0	48.2	47.0	49.2
	Rajasthan	46.7	50.1	46.6	49.6	48.4	55.4	51.1	65.4	68.4	67.3	74.3
	Chandigarh	82.0	79.5	99.4	99.3	102.8	102.3	110.4	99.4	99.3	102.8	102.3
	Delhi	60.5	53.7	66.1	57.6	67.6	59.1	67.8	66.3	57.8	67.7	59.2
2.	North-Eastern Region	28.1	30.6	27.6	32.0	27.2	53.2	26.8	44.9	49.3	45.2	71.2
	Arunachal Pradesh	15.7	22.3	14.5	22.1	15.8	27.4	17.0	24.3	31.8	22.7	34.3
	Assam	32.0	35.5	32.1	38.1	31.7	70.3	28.6	48.9	55.0	49.3	87.9
	Manipur	37.4	37.9	40.1	40.7	26.4	27.3	28.0	72.2	72.8	58.9	59.8
	Meghalaya	16.3	16.3	17.1	17.3	18.3	24.3	28.8	33.0	33.3	34.0	40.0
	Mizoram	23.3	26.0	24.1	29.0	26.4	36.2	26.4	43.8	48.7	48.5	58.4

1	2	3	4	5	6	7	8	9	10	11	12	13
	Nagaland	15.3	15.6	12.4	13.6	12.8	18.1	13.1	42.1	43.3	48.1	53.3
	Tripura	25.7	25.7	21.7	21.7	21.5	21.6	25.6	34.2	34.2	33.6	33.7
3.	Eastern Region	37.0	37.2	36.7	36.6	37.6	41.4	40.2	47.7	47.6	48.6	52.4
	Bihar	22.5	23.2	20.7	20.7	21.3	21.9	23.4	37.6	37.6	38.3	38.9
	Jharkhand	–	–	28.0	30.6	25.1	31.0	27.3	28.7	31.2	27.1	33.0
	Orissa	41.5	42.8	40.2	41.6	44.5	51.4	46.2	65.8	67.1	68.2	75.1
	Sikkim	15.1	15.2	14.4	14.5	16.0	22.5	17.2	31.7	31.7	29.9	36.4
	West Bengal	45.5	44.9	44.5	43.4	45.8	49.2	48.2	52.4	51.2	53.7	57.2
	Andaman & Nicobar	16.8	27.6	16.3	27.5	18.5	57.2	21.0	16.3	27.5	18.5	57.2
4.	Central Region	33.9	36.8	32.7	36.9	33.9	38.4	33.5	43.9	48.1	44.8	49.3
	Chattisgarh	–	–	38.5	49.9	44.0	54.2	39.1	39.4	50.8	46.6	56.8
	Madhya Pradesh	49.1	52.5	47.6	52.5	46.6	50.3	46.6	62.7	67.5	60.5	64.3
	Uttar Pradesh	28.2	30.9	28.3	31.9	29.9	34.3	30.4	40.3	43.9	41.7	46.1
	Uttaranchal	–	–	21.7	23.9	23.7	26.0	19.1	21.8	24.0	25.3	27.6
5.	Western Region	75.4	74.6	75.5	74.8	79.7	71.3	80.8	79.9	79.2	83.5	75.1
	Goa	23.8	25.4	26.1	27.3	25.3	28.2	23.2	29.5	30.7	29.2	32.1
	Gujarat	49.0	53.5	48.5	53.6	44.1	54.7	45.2	55.1	60.2	50.9	61.5
	Maharashtra	86.4	83.4	86.4	83.5	92.3	77.5	93.2	90.1	87.2	95.3	80.5
	Dadra & Nagar Haveli	18.8	135.6	14.3	135.2	20.9	189.0	23.5	14.3	135.2	20.9	189.0
	Daman & Diu	15.7	87.6	13.3	75.3	9.9	79.4	9.0	13.3	75.3	9.9	79.4
6.	Southern Region	66.2	66.8	66.6	66.8	64.6	68.9	65.0	75.2	75.3	72.9	77.1
	Andhra Pradesh	64.2	65.5	64.5	64.9	61.9	67.7	62.6	77.2	77.6	74.0	79.7

Contd....

1 2	3	4	5	6	7	8	9	10	11	12	13
Karnataka	63.3	65.5	61.8	61.8	61.6	68.9	60.9	67.6	68.5	68.4	75.7
Kerala	41.5	41.7	43.3	42.3	43.3	43.7	43.3	51.7	50.8	51.3	51.7
Tamil Nadu	88.6	87.5	90.6	90.6	85.4	88.5	86.5	97.6	97.5	91.9	95.1
Lakshadweep	7.4	9.1	10.4	11.8	7.9	9.6	5.1	10.4	11.8	7.9	9.6
Pondicherry	33.6	38.7	33.5	35.8	32.3	39.2	32.2	33.5	35.8	32.3	39.2
All India	56.0	56.0	56.7	56.7	58.4	58.4	59.4	64.3	64.3	65.6	65.6

@ Banks' State-wise i estment represent their holdings of state-level securities, such as. State Government loans and shares, bonds, debentures, etc. of Regional rural Banks. Co-operative institutions, State Electricity Boards, Municipal Corporations, Municipalies and Port Trusts, State financial Corporations, Housing Boards, State Industrial Development Corporations, Road Transport Corporations and other Government and *quasi*-Government bodies.

All-India investment *plus* credit-deposit ratio is worked out by excluding investments in Central Government and other securities not mentioned above.

— Not applicable.

Notes: 1. Deposits and credit (as per place of sanction and utilisation) data for 2000, 2001 and 2002 are based on BSR-1 and 2 surveys as on March 31.

2. The investment figures are based on BSR-5 survey as on March 31.

3. CD-ratio fro 2003 are based on BSR-7 survey as on March 31, 2003.

Appendix Table III 24
Ad vances to the Priority Sectors by Public Sector Banks
(As on the last reporting Friday)

Sector	No. of Accounts (in lakh)					Amount Outstanding (Rs. crore)				
	June 1969	March 2000	March 2001	March 2002@	March 2003@	June 1969	March 2000	March 2001	March 2002@	March 2003@
1	2	3	4	5	6	7	8	9	10	11
I. Agriculture	1.7	160	188	161	168	162 (5.4)	45.296 (14.3)	53.571 (15.7)	63.082 (15.9)	73.507 (15.3)
(i) Direct	1.6	157	185	157	164	40 (1.3)	34.247 (10.8)	38.137 (11.2)	44.908 (11.3)	51.799 (10.8)
(ii) Indirect	0.1	3	3	4	4	122 (4.0)	11.049 (3.5)	15.434 (4.5)	18.174 (4.6)	21.708 (4.5)
II. Small-scale industries	0.5	22	20	22	17	257 (8.5)	46.045 (14.6)	48.400 (14.2)	49.743 (12.5)	52.988 (11.1)
III. Other priority sector advances	0.4	81	80	83	79	22 (0.7)	30.816 (9.7)	40.791 (12.0)	53.712 (13.5)	71.448 (15.0)
IV. Total priority sector advances	2.6	265	288	269	268	441 (14.6)	1,27,478 (40.3)	1,49,116 (43.7)	1,71,185 (43.1)	2,03,095 (42.5)
V. Net Bank Credit	–	–	–	–	–	3,016	3,16,427	3,41,291	3,96,954	4,77899

@ Data are provisional:

\# Inclusive of advances to setting up industrial estates, funds provided to RRBs by sponsor banks, loan to software industries, food and agro processing sector, self-help group and venture capital.

Note: Figure in brackets represent percentages to net bank credit.

Appendix Table IV.1
Progress of Co-operative Credit Movement in India

(Amount in Rs. crore, ratio in per cent)

Sr.No.	*Type of Institution*	*Item*	*1999–2000*	*2000–01*	*2001–02 P*	*2002–03 P*
1	2	3	4	5	6	7
1.	Urban Co-operative Banks (UCBs)	Number	1,781	1,618	1,854	1,911
		Owned Funds	9,314	10,826	13,797	9,830
		Deposits	71,189	80,840	93,069	1,01,546
		Borrowings	1,475	2,069	N.A.	1,590
		Working Capital	90,301	1,03,042	1,15,596	1,11,746
		Loans Outstanding	45,995	54,389	62,060	64,880
		C-D Radio	65	67	67	64
2.	State Co-operative Bank (StCBs)	Number	29	30	30	29
		Owned Funds	4.911	5.837	6.323	N.A.
		Deposits	29.557	32.626	35.500	37.439
		Borrowings	10.859	11.693	11.550	12.079
		Working Capital	44.035	49.490	51.899	N.A.
		Loans Issured	37.368	34.307	34.287	38.318
		Loans Outstanding	25,709	29,861	32.111	34.861
		Recovery Performance (as per cent to demand)	83	84	81	N.A.
		C-D Ratio	87	92	90	93
3.	District Central Co-operative Banks (DCCBs)	Number	367	367	368	343
		Owned Funds	10.11[illegible]	12.180	14.148	N.A.
		Deposits	54,248	61,745	68,090	72,983
		Borrowings	14,658	16,935	18,818	18,157
		Working Capital	77,679	87,821	1,00,851	N.A.
		Loans Issued	49,619	45,016	55.998	50.482

1	2	3	4	5	6	7
		Loans Outstanding	44.538	52.478	59.269	59.338
		Recovery Performance (as per cent to demand)	69	67	66	N.A.
		C-D Ratio	82	85	87	N.A.
4.	State Co-operative Agriculture and Rural Development Banks (SCARDBs)	Number	19	20	20	20
		Owned Funds	2.702	3.034	2.753	N.A.
		Deposits	422	536	587	689
		Borrowings	12.390	13.413	14.875	13.861
		Working Capital	15.074	16.896	18.947	N.A.
		Loans Issued	2.532	2.586	2.746	2.631
		Loans Outstanding	11.565	12.553	14.172	13.870
		Recovery Performance (as per cent to demand)	62	58	55	N.A.
5.	Primary Co-operative Agriculture and Rural Development Banks (PCARDBs)	Number	755	732	768	768
		Owned Funds	1.379	1.628	2.502	N.A.
		Deposits	218	210	354	202
		Borrowings	7.647	8.294	10.292	7.857
		Working Capital	9.982	10.838	13.708	N.A.
		Loans Issued	1.819	1.865	2.045	1.696
		Loans Outstanding	7,611	8,295	10,010	8,960
		Recovery Performance (as per cent to demand)	58	53	46	N.A.

P Provisional. N.A. Not Available.

* Includes share capital & Statutory reserves and other free reserves & provisions not in the nature of outside liabilites.

Source: NABARD for Sr. No. 2 to 5.

Appendix Table IV.2
Performance as Proportion to Assets to Scheduled Urban Co-operative Banks (Continued)

(Per cent)

Sr. No.	Name of the Bank	Operating Profit		Net Profit		Interest Income	
		2001–02	2002–03	2001–02	2002–03	2001–02	2002–03
1	2	3	4	5	6	7	8
1.	Abhyudaya Co-op Bank Ltd.	1.80	3.07	0.69	0.67	9.89	9.84
2.	Ahmedabad Mercantile Co-op Bank Ltd.	3.38	3.54	0.64	0.73	11.89	11.62
3.	Akola Janata Commercial Co-op Bank Ltd.	1.79	1.97	0.42	0.51	10.54	10.60
4.	Akola Urban Co-op Bank Ltd.	1.81	1.57	0.53	0.66	13.96	13.89
5.	Amanath Co-op Bank Ltd. #	1.18	0.44	0.72	0.44	10.33	8.90
6.	AP Mahesh Co-op Urban Bank Ltd.	2.83	7.73	1.53	2.56	12.46	13.57
7.	Bassein Catholic Co-op Urban Bank Ltd.	2.13	2.21	1.28	1.28	9.99	9.64
8.	Bharat Co-op Bank (Mumbai) Ltd.	2.11	2.57	0.99	0.97	10.89	10.50
9.	Bharati Sahakari Bank Ltd.	–	1.08	–	0.32	–	8.95
10.	Bombay Mercantile Co-op Bank Ltd.	–0.07	1.28	–3.20	1.28	6.95	5.73
11.	Charminar Co-op Bank Ltd.	–7.50	–2.30	–20.22	–3.03	3.89	3.54
12.	Charotar Nagarik Sahakari Bank Ltd. #	–0.09	0.62	–0.87	–19.62	13.26	7.58
13.	Citizencredit Co-op Bank Ltd.	1.74	1.58	0.88	1.01	9.15	8.03
14.	Co-operative Bank of Ahmedabad	–2.17	–2.97	–2.17	–6.92	8.63	6.81
15.	Cosmos Co op Bank Ltd.	2.49	3.17	1.13	1.07	11.11	11.49
16.	Dombivli Nagari Sahakari Bank Ltd.	2.22	2.19	0.88	0.87	10.16	9.81
17.	Goa Urban Co-op Bank Ltd.	2.45	2.87	0.43	0.46	11.08	9.23
18.	Greater Bombay Co-op Bank Ltd.	4.49	2.38	2.02	1.41	9.35	9.53
19.	Ichalkaranji Janata Sahakari Bank Ltd.	2.18	1.70	0.97	0.85	10.58	9.61
20.	Indian Mercantile Co-op Bank Ltd.	0.86	1.71	0.86	1.71	11.85	9.47

1	2	3	4	5	6	7	8
21.	Jalgaon Janata Sahakari Bank Ltd.	2.17	1.76	0.64	0.58	8.45	8.27
22.	Janalaxmi co-op Bank Ltd.	2.56	2.31	0.29	0.43	16.93	16.48
23.	Janata Sahakari Bank Ltd.	0.64	0.18	–2.27	–1.33	7.76	6.90
24.	Janakalyan Sahakari Bank Ltd.	2.32	1.83	0.58	0.46	11.58	10.90
25.	Kalupur Commercial Co-op Bank Ltd.	4.16	4.16	1.73	1.75	12.31	10.86
26.	Kalyan Janata Sahakari Bank Ltd.	2.32	2.55	0.82	0.50	7.46	7.98
27.	Kapol Co-op Bank Ltd.	1.91	1.51	0.55	0.89	9.09	7.82
28.	Karad Urban Co-op Bank Ltd.	2.91	1.75	1.43	0.83	10.20	9.09
29.	Khamgaon Urban Co-op Bank Ltd.	2.12	1.25	0.60	0.41	14.30	14.09
30.	Madhavpura Mercantile Co-op Bank Ltd #	–1.85	–1.91	–7.51	–1.91	1.42	1.03
31.	Mahanagar Co-op Bank Ltd.	2.44	1.30	0.13	0.31	11.65	9.91
32.	Mandvi Co-op Bank Ltd.	1.61	1.00	0.58	0.54	10.09	9.10
33.	Mapusa Urban Co-op Bank of Goa Ltd. #	–3.81	–1.95	–7.07	–4.19	5.55	5.17
34.	Mehsana Urban Co-op Bank Ltd.	1.91	3.46	1.33	0.87	12.59	14.13
35.	Nagar Urban Co-op Bank Ltd.	1.19	2.05	0.85	1.07	13.97	13.80
36.	Nagpur Nagrik Sahakari Bank Ltd.	4.34	2.34	0.46	0.54	10.92	9.22
37.	Nasik Merchant's Co-op Bank Ltd.	2.66	2.08	2.11	0.60	11.10	10.56
38.	New India Co-op Bank Ltd.	2.09	2.76	1.73	1.95	10.11	9.87
39.	North Kanara G.S.B. Co-op Bank Ltd.	1.47	1.71	0.90	0.98	10.08	9.62
40.	Nutan Nagarik Sahakari Bank Ltd.	1.74	3.11	1.46	1.97	10.37	10.10
41.	Parsik Janata Sahakari Bank Ltd.	3.45	3.01	1.83	1.68	9.63	9.12
42.	Pravara Sahakari Bank Ltd. #	–	3.27	–	0.44	–	11.80
43.	Punjab & Maharashtra Co-op Bank Ltd.	2.06	1.70	1.31	1.29	10.77	10.20
44.	Rajkot Nagrik Sahakari Bank Ltd.	6.67	2.22	0.83	1.12	8.06	7.84

Contd....

1	2	3	4	5	6	7	8
45.	Rupee Co-op Bank Ltd.	0.85	–1.54	–5.70	–7.47	9.33	6.43
46.	Sangli Urban Co-op Bank Ltd.	1.91	1.85	0.52	0.33	10.36	9.23
47.	Saraswat Co-op Bank Ltd.	2.19	2.10	0.55	0.57	8.15	7.95
48.	Sardar Bhiladwala Pardi People's Co-op Bank Ltd.	0.49	1.03	0.46	0.04	9.30	9.15
49.	Shamrao Vithal Co-op Bank Ltd.	1.77	2.13	1.06	0.96	10.52	10.08
50.	Shikshak Sahakari Bank Ltd.	1.99	0.69	–0.09	–1.92	7.20	6.46
51.	Solapur Janata Sahakari Bank Ltd.	–	1.70	–	0.52	–	11.77
52.	Surat People's Co-op Bank Ltd.	2.90	3.42	0.79	1.08	10.35	10.72
53.	Thane Bharat Sahakari Bank Ltd.	–	1.77	–	0.97	–	9.39
54.	Thane Janata Sahakari Bank Ltd.	1.95	2.20	1.60	1.57	10.02	10.17
55.	Vasavi Co-operative Urban Bank Ltd. #	0.39	0.26	–7.31	0.26	16.53	14.13
56.	Visnagar Nagrik Sahakari Bank Ltd.	0.42	–4.63	0.39	–41.12	25.38	8.50
57.	Zoroastrian Co-op Bank Ltd.	–	1.93	–	0.48	–	9.70
	Total	1.52	1.37	–0.88	–1.14	9.40	8.58

CII OPENS 8-POINT REFORMS PLAN FOR MAHARASHTRA

BS Regional Bureau In Mumbai May 12, 2003 13:21 Ist

Fiscal prudence, power sector reforms and developing Mumbai as the country's first international offshore financial centre figure in an right-point reforms programme for achieving an increased state domestic product growth in Maharasthra.

The agenda prepared by the Confederation of the Indian Industry was announced at an interaction of Members of Parliament from Maharashtra belonging to various political parties in New Delhi on Thursday

CII Chairman (Maharashtra) S M Trehan emphasised the need for judicious management of the state's finances to facilitate rapid economic advances.

"Short and long term measures recommended include curbing of off-budget borrowings and guarantees, restructuring of the Maharashtra State Electricity Board, greater control over non-development expenditure, rationalizing and proper realization of user charges, discontinuation of the cotton monopoly scheme, infrastructure development and privatisation of ports, roads and power," Trehan said.

He said the captive power policy could play a significant role in reducing the acute power shortage in Maharashtra. The agenda also emphasises the need for a concrete plan for the development of Mumbai city as India' first international offshore financial centre.

Easing of the Coastal Regulatory Zone norms in a city like Mumbai where availability of land is very less would boost the housing industry, the report said.

CII has highlighted the need to look at integrated working of various agencies like the Brihanmumbai Municipal Corporation. Thane Municipal Corporation, Maharashtra State Road Development Corporation and the Mumbai Metropolitan Region Development Authority.

Maharashtra's competitive advantage over other states in the areas of biotechnology, agriculture and tourism should see these sectors being promoted jointly through public-private participation, the agenda said.

The CII has sought speedy implementation of the Value Added Tax regime. "CII feels that Maharashtra's announcement of its decision to introduce VAT by June 1, 2003, is a powerful signal that the government is committed to rationalising the system of taxes for the long term good of the economy.

"However certain provisions of the bill may require a review to make them more industry friendly," Trehan said.

Revival of the manufacturing sector, labour reforms and repealing the Urban Land Ceiling (Regulations) Act are also suggested.

13

COMMENTS AND OBSERVATIONS ON THE TECHNICAL SESSION ON AGENDA FOR REMOVAL OF REGIONAL IMBALANCES AND BANKING SECTOR REFORMS

K. Ramesha

BACKDROP

Globalization has many dimensions, mostly familiar of many such dimensions are trade, capital, labour and knowledge. While these are essentially economic dimensions, there are other dimensions to globalization as well, having to do with, for instance globalization of civil society. Broadly speaking, there are those who consider globalization to be a panacea for all of society's ills and there are those who regard globalization as merely the latest stage in capitalism. However, there seems to be a broad agreement amongst scholars that the rapidly changing global economy provides both opportunities as well as challenges, not all of which can be foreseen due to the way in which global economic forces are unfolding. The progress of globalization has undoubtedly affected the balance of relationships between the State, labour and business and has brought new opportunities for wealth creation and prosperity together with new insecurities and inequalities. The economic reform agenda set against the backdrop of globalization is dominating the socio-economic-cultural scenario in recent years.

BALANCED REGIONAL DEVELOPMENT

While the growth rate of the Indian economy has been rather commendable during the post reforms period, there are apprehension that this growth has not trickled-down across the states in an equitable manner. There are also views that the growth (in GDP) should result in "development" the essence of which is improved quality of living. Development is not purely a subject matter of economics. Though the concept of development itself has undergone change, one of its important dimensions, viz., disparities in development levels across the regions/states as also socio-economic groups has assumed greater significance in the present liberalized environment. While 'growth' was the focal point of the policy framework of many countries in the past, of late, the policy makers as well as researchers have realized that the growth can not be sustained in the long run with the increasing regional imbalances. Therefore, balanced regional development has to be viewed not just from economic growth angle, but also from the angle of 'human' dimension of development. The balanced regional development does not necessarily mean equal development of all the regions or states. It essentially means, ensuring equal opportunities for the people of different regions as also within the region to have the benefits of development. In other words, balanced regional development aims at reducing regional disparities in living standards. At the state level it is noteworthy that the Government of Maharashtra in its recent budget has proposed regional financial packages like Vidarbha Vikas Package (318.30 Crores), Marathwada Vikas Package (588 Crores), Konkan Vikas Package (300 Crores), Khandesh Vikas Package (287.96 Crores) and the Drought Prone Areas, Hilly Areas and Western Ghat Development Package (452.56 Crores). These programs if implemented effectively should reduce intra-region disparity.

INTER-STATE DISPARITIES IN LEVELS OF DEVELOPMENT

Although the process of reforms officially began in the nineties, the compulsions as well as indications towards the same were very much evident in late eighties. It is an acknowledged fact that the growth rate of GDP during the post reforms period has been impressive the available indications suggest that economy's growth momentum will be sustained in the years to come. According to the advance estimate of the CSO, the economy is likely to grow by 6.9 per cent in 2004–05. While everything seems to be rosy at the rosy at the aggregate level with return of 'feel-good factor', Dr R.P. Kurulkari analysis of the impact of economic reforms on the development levels of states is quite interesting and revealing. His discussion along with empirical evidences essentially conveys that the inter-state disparities have widened during the post-reforms period. For instance the coefficient of variation with respect to net per capita state domestic product, which was 26.37 and 28.12 per cents for time points 1981 and 1991 (pre-reform period) respectively, increased to 33.39 per cent in 2001 (post-reforms period). The forward states as a block, which showed an average annual growth rate of 5.2 per cent during pre-reform period, improved its growth rate to 6.3 per cent during post reforms period. On the other hand the growth rate for backward states declined from 4.9 to 3 per cent during the same period. Perhaps the picture may marginally change if the post-reforms period is redefined to cover data up to 2004. It must be remembered that in this paper post reforms period is restricted to 1990–91 to 1997–98. The author has also pointed out that there are pockets of poverty (backward districts) even within forward states. Further, the author also observes that the proportion of people living below poverty line has come down across the states during post reforms period. Perhaps, a more pragmatic picture of inter-state inequalities in regard to development may be obtained by suing indices of human development. The analysis of Dr Kurulkar clearly brings out that though inter-state inequalities continued during post-reforms period, the value of all India Human Development Index (HDI) is on an increasing trend. But what is worrisome is the states, which occupied low ranking in terms of HDI during pre-reforms, have continued to occupy more or less the same positions during post-reforms period also. Further, the paper reveals that low HDI states also have low per capita income, with a couple of exceptions like Kerala. The agenda and the action plan suggested by the author are indeed in the right direction. But, it is disheartening to note that fiscal position of most of the states have worsened in the recent past and I am afraid that the states may not be in a position to carry forward the policies and programs aimed at reforms as well as backward area development.

STATE LEVEL FISCAL REFORMS: NEED OF THE HOUR

Let me touch upon the fiscal health of the states at this stage. Though the fiscal deterioration of states began much later than that of the center, the fiscal stress of some of the states are more acute and an important constraint in their development. The revenue account of states has been continuously in deficit since 1987–88. The deterioration in the revenue accounts of states has been more pronounced from the late nineties. As a proportion of GDP the revenue deficit of the states which increased from 0.3 per cent in 1987–88 to 1.1 per cent in 1996–97, shot up to 2.5 per cent in 1998–99 following mainly the revision of pay scales. It is hovering around 2.6 per cent now. The share of revenue deficit in fiscal deficit increased from an average of 25 per cent during the period 1990–95 to 48.6 per cent during 1995–2000 and further to 54 per cent in 2002–03. More importantly, the share of non-developmental expenditure to total, which was 24.8 per cent in 1990–91, increased to 32.1 per cent in 2003–04 and expected to touch 36.2 per cent in 2004–05. The outstanding liabilities of the states as a proportion of GDP, which was 18.1 per cent in 1994–95 shot up to 29.2 per cent in 2003–04 and is expected to touch 29.4 per cent in 2004–05. In other words, the gross borrowings of the state governments has gone up from Rs. 2569 crores in 1990–91 to Rs. 50, 521 crores in 2003–04. The proportion of non-developmental expenditure to the total of all the states, which was 24.8 per cent in 1990–91, has grown to 36.2 as per estimates for 2004–05. In other words, the share of developmental expenditure to total, which was around 70 per cent in 1990–91, has come down to around 51 per cent in 2004–05. In the state of Maharashtra 22, 15 and 22 per cents of the total revenue expenditure is spent on repayment of debt, servicing of debts and general services respectively.

Twelfth Finance Commission (TFC) has made far-reaching recommendation liking debt relief (swapping of high cost debts with low cost debts) to the enactment of fiscal responsibility legislation. Only five states have enacted Fiscal Responsibility Legislation till 2003–04. State Governments will have to go for market borrowings and if they can not raise funds at cheaper rates, then they will be compelled to borrow from NSSF at 9.5 per cent. In view of the above, it may be concluded that the fiscal health of the states in India is far from satisfaction. Unless the state governments improve their fiscal condition, the developmental programs would continue to suffer. Therefore, the starting point of reforms at the state level invariably has to begin with fiscal reforms. It is heartening to note that TFC and centre have released the road map in this direction.

ECONOMIC DEVELOPMENT AND FINANCIAL SECTOR

The importance of Financial System in the process of development needs no emphasis. The relationship between financial sector development and economic growth is well recognized. Financial system contributes to the economic development process through four transformation mechanisms, viz.,

(a) Liability-asset transformation (converting deposits into loans).

(b) Size transformation (providing large loans by pooling small numerous deposits).

(c) Maturity transformation (offering alternative forms of deposits to savers in accordance with their liquidity preferences and providing loans of different maturities) and

(d) Risk transformation (risk distribution through diversification thereby reducing the risk for savers).

As a sequel to economic reforms, the reforms in the financial sector reforms was initiated in 1992 with the acceptance of the recommendations of the Report of the Committee on Financial System (1991, also known as Narasimham Committee). The roadmap for reforms in banking sector, one of the significant players of the financial system was more clearer after the acceptance of the recommendations of the Report of the Committee on Banking Sector Reforms (1998, Narasimham II). The ongoing reforms have not only resulted in financial sector consolidation, but also ensured a competitive environment, a must for improving efficiency. Today, the global standards in banking in terms of prudential standards as enunciated in Basel-I and Basel-II are followed by financial intermediaries in India.

Dr. V.S. Kulkarni in his paper has tracked the developments in financial system. His paper touches upon the critical challenges before the banks in the fast-changing environment. The time-bound action plan suggested by Dr Kulkarni is also interesting. While the performance of the banking system in terms of profitability and volumes has been quite commendable during the post-reforms period, there are issues, which can not be conveniently ignored. For instance, the performance of RRBs is an issue of concern. Similarly, rural credit cooperatives have weakened during the post-reforms period. The performance of Urban Cooperative Banks (UCBs) is rather dismal. Let me give you a feel of the credit cooperative sector, which supplied more than 50 per cent of the rural credit during pre-reforms period.

As on March 31, 2003, 5 out of 30 SCBs, 102 out of 367 DCCBs, 43, 511 out of 98, 247 PACS, 10 out of 20 SCARDBs and 469 out of 768 PCARDBs incurred losses which together amounted to Rs. 7,734 crores (NABARD Annual Report 2003–04). The gross NPAs of SCBs and DCCBs as per cent of loans outstanding worked out to be 13.4 and 19.7 as on March 2002 (RBI, Report on Trend and Progress 2003). A quick inspection of 10 SCBs and 88 DCCBs by NABARD during 2003–04 revealed that some of the weaknesses that continued to affect the functioning of these banks were improper application/ implementation of income recognition and asset classification norms, inadequate risk management strategies, deficient internal checks and controls and poor credit monitoring. Further, if one looks at rural cooperatives from a non-financial angle, then also the picture is rather bleak. For instance, the elected management of 41 per cent of State Cooperative Banks, 37 per cent of State Cooperative Agricultural and Rural Development Banks, 21 per cent of the

District Central Cooperative Banks and 8 per cent of Primary Cooperative Agricultural and Rural Development Banks stood superseded as on March 2000.

The Urban Cooperative Banking (UCBs) segment, which was considered as one of the robust and fast expanding segments of the banking system in early nineties, has now become one the weakest with intermittent cases of failures/irregularities. A host of factors may be responsible for this, which may include increasing competition, tightening prudential standards and supervision and regulatory standards, multiple control, etc. In fact, the Committee on Financial System (1991) had indeed lauded the performance and progress of urban banking segment in the early nineties. Today, there are apprehensions as to whether these entities will be able to survive in the increasingly competitive environment. Based on the new classification, the number of UCBs classified as "weak" stood at 944 as on March 31, 2003 and 142 of these could not comply with the stipulated minimum capital requirements. The scheduled UCBs as a segment recorded negative net profit during the last three years. During 2003–04 alone, liquidation proceedings have been initiated in respect of 23 UCBs, apart from descheduling two scheduled UCBs. The rate of growth of deposits was just 3.3 per cent (as against 10.6 per cent for the previous year) during the first half of 2003–2004 Credit growth, in tandem, declined by 6.1 per cent in sharp contrast to an increase of 2.8 per cent last year. The relatively low deposit growth also speaks of the falling public confidence of the general public in cooperative banks, particularly UCBs due to the recent untoward incidents. However, nearly 45 per cent of the UCBs accounting for 55 per cent of the deposit base of the sector are considered financially sound (Mid-term Review of Annual Policy, 2004).

An important dimension of banking system in the country is inter-state disparities in banking development. The inter-state disparity in institutional credit becomes glaring if one uses crude parameters like ratio of institutional agricultural credit to value of agricultural production, institutional credit as per cent of production from SSI sector or for that matter number of bank branches per lakh population. Simplest of them, perhaps could be CD ratio. Therefore, it is imperative that first institutional credit agencies like banks, RRBs, cooperatives are strengthened in backward states/ regions. It will be undoubtedly a challenging task. After all, one can expect banks to contribute meaningfully for the upliftment of deprived sections of the society only when these banks are strong. It must be remembered that compelling financial intermediaries to lend to sectors they deem risky, would be too great a risk a Government can take in the present era.

I take this opportunity to thank Dr Jugale and his colleagues for giving me this wonderful opportunity. My congratulations to Dr Kurul kar and Dr Kulkarni for their excellent and lucid presentations.

Thank you, one and all.

14

AGENDA FOR FISCAL REFORMS AT THE STATE LEVEL IN INDIA

M. Narasimhulu

PRELUDE

It is inappropriate to discuss the fiscal reforms at the states level without having an idea of the reforms process introduced at the Central Government level. India is neither a unitary type of government like USA. Therefore the situation of India is referred to as the Union of States and is Quasi Federal. The Central government has many controls on state governments. Indian states are not as independent as the states in America. Therefore the policies pursued at the central level will have its impact on the state governments. Therefore it is appropriate to give a brief overview of the reform process at the center and the reasons to initiate the reforms.

INDIAN ECONOMY ON THE EVE OF IMPLEMENTATION OF ECONOMIC REFORMS

The policies of Jawaharlal Nehru and Indira Gandhi laid foundation of economic development and social justice but cannot answer to the challenges faced by Indian Economy by the year 1990.

After 40 years of planning development efforts (1950–51 to 1990–91). We have faced a situation as stagnant and sick economy with poverty, unemployment, inflation, black money, rampant public debt (both internal & external), fiscal inblances, balance of payment, disequilibrium, regional imbalances in the levels of development, smuggling, corruption, inefficiency and scarcity of essential goods. In short by June, 1991 India reached a stage where the economy was on the verge of collapse. Foreign exchange balances were just sufficient to pay import bill for a week or so. Not been able to meet foreign debt payment commitment, inflation was in the two digit. New job opportunities were not rising. Foreign lenders and N.R.I's lost their confidence on our country. Capital was moving out of our country. We were about to default our foreign loans. There was despair and gloom all around.

Before Industrial Revolution the India's share in the world manufacturing output was 17.6%, U.K. share was 9.[illegible]% and U.S.A share was 2.3%.

By 1900 the share of India in the world trade declined to 1.7%, U.K. and U.S.A. shares have increased to 18.5% and 23.6% respectively.

During 1871 to 1947 rate of growth of India was only 1.5% per year whereas U.K. and U.S.A. was far higher. Rate of savings in India in 1947 was just 5%.

In 1950 India's Industrial sector was bigger than Taiwan or South Korea. Share of our exports in world's markets was higher than that of China, South Korea, Singapore, Indonesia and Malaysia. The level of poverty was more in the above countries than India but as on today all these countries have passed us. These countries export more than what we do. Their industry is more competitive than ours. They have higher level of foreign exchange reserves. All these economies (except China) have eradicated poverty and reached the status of middle income countries among world nations. Their per capita income is as atleast thrice high than ours. Their literacy rate and health care facility is higher than ours. On an average their people enjoyed higher quality of life.

WAY INDIA LAGGED BEHIND

India has followed the path of composite mixed economy. It has imposed several controls on production. Licensing restrictions along with high protection walls. Our companies produced goods of poor quality which can be sold in domestic market and have little acceptance in the world market. Many of the large companies in India imported more than they exported. This situation led to large trade deficit which in its turn led to costly foreign borrowings which in its turn led to increasing foreign debt which caused increasing interest payments. This led to increasing money supply which led to increase in demand more than domestic production causing to increase in prices on one side and increase in imports on the other.

Over the years our Taxation lost is buoyancy. There was rampant tax evasion. Tax rates were high which led to evasion causing emergence of black money. Black money led to operation of parallel economy, which led to ineffectiveness of government policies.

So far as expenditure policies are concerned more was allocated to public sector increase in wages, salaries, interest payments, defence expenditure led to less allocation to productive sectors such as agriculture, irrigation and education, health etc.

Due to licences, high protection and high import duties industrial sector could not grow fast. Hence employment has not increased substantially. Poverty continued. Late Mr. P.V. Narasimha Rao, the then Prime Minister in his address to Parliament on 9th March, 1992 stated that foreign exchange reserves had declined to a very low level by June, 1991. 2.4 Billion loan was drawn from IMF. During July 1990 to January 1991 the IMF and World Bank told us no fresh aid will be given until basic reforms were undertaken. The situation, the country faced by 1991 did not give any option but to get assistance from IMF and World Bank.

In view of the issues discussed above the government of India has initiated economic reforms under the Prime Ministership of late Mr. P.V. Narasimha Rao and the present Prime Minister (then Finance Minister) Dr. Manmohan Singh in June, 1991.

THE AIM OF ECONOMIC REFORMS

The implementation of the reforms which is generally referred to as new economic policy led to structural adjustments, scrapping of industrial licenses, abolition of MRTP and FERA. Welcoming the foreign capital above 50% equity in industry and 100% equity in export oriented industry. Trade Policy liberalized to gain from globalization and to attract foreign capital. To raise revenue to government kit tax rates both direct and indirect have been slashed. Efforts have been to decrease support to public sector as well as disinvestment in loss making public sector undertakings. User changes having proposed to be increased to meet the cost.

In short the main aim of new economic policy is to transform the country into strong, stable, attractive, efficient, competitive and have prestigious place for India in the world economies by becoming worlds economic giant. It is expected that the rate of growth of industry will be around 12% per annum. It is felt to encourage private sector in the areas where they have the ability to invest and manage. In sectors like oil, power, steel machine tools where both private and foreign investors will invest so that government can spend less on them which enables the government to spend more on social sectors like drinking water, sanitation, health, housing, education. In the changed circumstances public sector could concentrate on areas like agriculture, irrigation, environment, employment generation and poverty reduction programmes.

IMPACT OF CENTRAL FISCAL CRISIS ON STATES FINANCES

The problems of the central government are reflected at the states level as the frame work of fiscal federation with in which India functions makes center states resource flows as an important component of state budgets (almost accounting for 1/3 or more of state budgets). Recent studies point to the fact that the center is attempting to cope with its fiscal crisis by passing on the burden of fiscal adjustment to the states through lower center state transfers (growth prospects recede as macroeconomic situation slipped out of control).

One important development on the economic front since the 1980's has been the emergence of government fiscal crisis. The problem of the imbalance in state finances between revenue and expenditure has serious implications for the pursuit of development strategies at the state level. The states have a greater role to play in providing overall objectives of economic development and social justice in the states.

STATES FINANCES AN OVERVIEW

Stagnant revenues and growing public expenditure is seen in the states. Resource mobilization efforts of the states is not adequate. The central government policies have far bearing on state finances. The increase in the salaries of the staff of Central Government due to implementation of 5th Pay Commission report forced many state governments to appoint Pay Commissions to its employees and give higher scales. The UGC scales to college teachers, D.A. revision for each six months by central government forced the state governments to incur large establishment expenditure. All these have telling effect on adverse financial situation of states. At present some states are not been able to pay salaries to its employees unless overdraft is taken. It is found that at the aggregate level the states at present on their own account for only a third of the total tax and non-tax revenues collected in the country. Whereas their share in total public spending is more than 50%. The attempts to bridge this gap are problematic as there are some limits—partly political—to the extent to which the taxing powers are exercised at the level of states.

The revenue sources of states are circumscribed by the Constitutional provisions, which lay down specific areas of the economy where states are empowered to levy taxes as experience has shown, what the states are Constitutionally empowered to do it is not always translated into appropriate tax legislation. For example, among direct taxes the important category of agriculture income falls within the purview of the states fiscal policy but the failure of the most states in the country to tax this important source has been one of the most politicized issues in India's public finance since Independence. At the time of Independence it was the land revenue which was contributing major charge to the states exchequer, but today it has lost its prestigious position and still remains controversial and the power of farm lobbies in influencing policy in most of the larger states reveal the problems in reconciling economic rationale with political realities.

The introduction of prohibition in some states has also resulted in loss of Revenue. The major revenue source at present in the states budgets is indirect taxes, which have their own limits. The cascade effect of sales tax and excise duties in particular and the resulting inflationary potential of this taxes restricts their use as source of revenue. Non-tax revenues account for a very small percentage of total revenue receipts at the level of states.

On the expenditure side rising levels of Revenue Expenditure has become almost an inbuilt feature of state budgets, partly in response to pressure from various interest groups according to the report of the National Institute of Public Finance and Policy two thirds of the non-merit subsidies are states sponsored. Payment of subsidies to farmers (through subsidized supply of power, water and fertilizers *etc*) has become another politicized issue where economic factors are not the sold determinants of such expenditures. For example, many state governments announced the supply of power to farmers in their election manifestos. Supply of rice, kerosene at subsidized prices through network of fair price shops. Supply of Jawar Roti for Rs. 1/- etc., though important from the view point of ensuring food security to the economically disadvantaged, as its adverse impact on state finances which cannot be overlooked.

Attempts to bridge the gap between inadequate revenues and increasing public expenditure have led the states into a fiscal crisis similar to that of the central government. The combined revenue deficit of the states is estimated at Rs. 48326 crores which works out to 1.8% GDP. Same way the gross fiscal deficit of all the states together is Rs. 116175 crores which works out to 4.2% of GDP. This speaks of the fiscal crisis at the state level. Many of the state governments are seeking overdrafts from Reserve Bank of India regularly.

No doubt the states have access to the share in the central governments pool of direct taxes. They also receive grants from the center. However, both these are declining in recent years. In the light of the discussion above there is a need for state governments to undertake reforms to solve their fiscal crisis along with other reforms. Therefore there is a need to suggest agenda for fiscal reforms at the state level.

AGENDA FOR FISCAL REFORMS AT THE STATES LEVEL

1. Expenditure Reform
2. Revenue Reform
3. Public Debt Reform
4. Reform in Deficits
5. Power Sector Reform
6. Debt GDP Ratio.

EXPENDITURE REFORM

In the year 2000–2001 state governments taken together spent 16% of India's GDP. Of this 68% is funded by Revenue and remaining 32% by current borrowings. 90% of the expenditure is on revenue account, remaining 10% is on capital account. The larger revenue expenditure is because of salaries (37%) interest payments (18%) and pensions (9%). During 1990's state governments expenditure grew annually at the rate of 13% per annum. It is in line with the GDP growth. During the decade 1990 the pension grew at a higher rate (22%) followed by interest payments (18%).

Most of the current revenue is just sufficient for revenue expenditure. In some years it is falling short of revenue receipts. Therefore the revenue expenditure over and above revenue receipts is met by receipts on capital accout.

SALARIES AND PENSIONS

Most public sector employees in India are greatly overpaid relative to their private sector counter parts. Due to 5th Pay Commission, pay scales the ratio of the average public to private sector wage is now 233% up, from 192% a decade earlier. Even this varies slightly from state to state. Due to this government is incurring huge amounts on non-plan expenditure. The details pertaining to the above discussion is given in Table 1.

Table 1
Statement Showing the Ratio of Average Wages in the Public and Private Sector 1993–1994 and 1999–2000

Sl. No.	*Name of the State*	*1993–94*	*1999–2000*
1.	Andhra Pradesh	2.35	2.13
2.	Bihar	1.41	2.14
3.	Gujarat	1.91	2.05
4.	Haryana	1.84	1.93
5.	Karnataka	2.11	2.07
6.	Kerala	1.78	2.06
7.	Madhya Pradesh	2.08	2.19
8.	Maharashtra	1.53	1.89
9.	Orissa	1.88	2.30
10.	Punjab	2.17	2.56
11.	Rajasthan	1.72	2.70
12.	Tamil Nadu	2.23	2.46
13.	Uttar Pradesh	2.27	2.58
14.	West Bengal	1.96	2.17
15.	All India	1.92	2.33

Source: NSSO 50th and 55th Round Employment—-Unemployment schedule data.

The variation was highest in Andhra Pradesh at 2.35 in the year 1993–94. However in the year 1999–2000 it is the Rajasthan state where this ratio was highest.

Another reason for the increasing expenditure on salaries is because of higher scales and payment of dearness allowances for each six months. For example take the case of primary school teachers whose salaries have increased several times.

For example Orissa's cost of living allowance is at 51% of basic salary. It is below the government of India's which was 59%. Some states have reduced other allowances such as leave encashment. The salaries also vary from state to state. In some states contract teachers are appointed without loosing quality the state governments are saving on this count. In the year 1995 the state basic salary of the primary school teacher was the highest in Tamilnadu whereas in Punjab it is highest in 2003. Thus some states in India implemented reforms on salary expenditure with a view to reduce non-plan expenditure by not appointing permanent teachers, but only appointing adhoc, part time and contract teachers. The details pertaining to the variation in basic pay of primary school teachers in some states is given in Table 2.

Table 2
Statement Showing the Starting Basic Pay of a Primary School Teacher in Some States During 1995–2003

Sl. No.	*State*	*Basic Salary per month in Ruppes*	
		1995	*2003*
1.	Andhra Pradesh	1,016	3,750
2.	Karnataka	1,040	3,300
3.	Orissa	1,080	3,600
4.	Punjab	1,200	4,550
5.	Tamil Nadu	1,200	4,500
6.	Uttar Pradesh	1,100	4,500

Source: World Bank 1996 'A' various state governments.

It is the salary expenditure which is consuming most of the revenue receipts. Therefore state governments in India are undertaking expenditure reforms on the count of salaries and pensions. Orissa and Karnataka have offered voluntary retirement packages to their civil servants but the civil servants were reluctant to opt for it. Goa is the only state which has succeeded in retrenching about 2,000 civil servants that is about 5% of the total civil service. Even here, people were aged around 55 years and about 40 to 45% of them have been replaced by new younger employees. This measure gave very nominal saving to the state government.

The government of Orissa has shown that a large number of aided institutions has not a single student pass the final examination. Thus the reforms on salary and pension are partial. Therefore down sizing and wage decompression is the best package. In Andhra Pradesh it is estimated core civil service have declined by an annual average of 2.4% in the past three year. As a percentage of GSDP salaries are estimated to have fallen in Andhra Pradesh from 5.5% in 2000–2001 to 5.2% in 2001–2002 and 5% in 2002–2003 and 4% in 2006–2007. Taking all states together since 1997 state employees strength shows an overall marginal reduction of 0.7%.

Pensions are a rapidly mounting liability. About 7.5% of total expenditure is spent on pensions. The annual average in pension spending was 30% between 95–96 and 2000–2001 making the pensions fastest growing expenditure item in state budgets. In this context also two types of reforms have been envisaged. One is structural reforms to enable shifting to a cheaper and less fiscal risky defined contribution (DC). Government of India has announced this for new civil servants. Several state governments also expressed their desire in favour of DC scheme. Maharashtra, Tamilnadu and Himachal Pradesh have opted for this. This measure will not reduce to a great extent in the revenue expenditure of the state governments immediately but it will help only in the long run.

The second type of reforms in pension is parametric reform. To contain the cost of the current pay as you go system. This is taken up on Tamilnadu, but its employees went on strike against this.

PATTERN OF EXPENDITURE

The growth rate in aggregate expenditure is budged to decline from 17.3% in 2002–2003 to 10.3% in 2003–2004, of this 60% is the revenue expenditure and remaining 40% will be capital expenditure, i.e., revenue expenditure would account for 13.9% of GDP in 2003–2004 whereas it was 14.4% in 2002–2003. The decrease in this is primarily due to slow down in interest payments and lower provision for energy. The decrease in capital expenditure is mainly due to a lower order of increase in payment of loans to the center and an absolute decline in loans and advances extended by the state governments. The development expenditure has slightly decreased from 56% in 2002–2003 to 55.1% in 2003–2004.

REVENUE EXPENDITURE

The Revenue Expenditure was 12.8% in 2002–2003 which has been planned to decrease to 7.7%. However non-development expenditure account for the major portion (62%) of the increase in revenue expenditure in 2003–2004 within the non-developmental component the growth in interest payments is budged to decline from 18.7% in 2002–2003 to 11.8% in 2003–2004 of the development component the provision for energy show a substantial decline of 15.4 in the budget estimates for 2003–2004 in relation to an increase of 6.3% in 2002–2003. However provisions for Rural development are budgeted to increase by 29.6% in 2003–2004 on top of rise of 22.7% in the previous year. The expenditure on education is also budgeted to increase by 7.2% in 2003–2004 which is slightly lower than that of 8% in 2002–2003.

In short the revenue expenditure aims at decreasing allocation to interest payments, energy and education and increase to rural development.

REFORMS IN THE EXPENDITURE ON SUBSIDIES

Subsidies have proved difficult to cut due to political reasons. The power subsidy is the largest state government subsidy which is difficult to reduce it. However it is suggested to rationalize and reduce it, by providing free supply of power to the marginal and small farmers. Irrigation and education are also having highest subsidies. Many states provide subsidies for fertilizers, agricultural machinery, public transport, housing and food. Subsidies paid from the budget have more or less remained stagnant as a percentage of GDP, actual loss increased from 0.6% of GDP in 1992–93 to almost 1.4% in 1999–2000. The ratio of subsidy paid to losses made has fallen from about 0.8 in the mid 1990's to less than half. Losses are financed by borrowings.

Power sector loses have come down as a percentage of GDP in recent years due to introduction of reforms in the power sector. Due to theft of power and rapid increase in generation in unit cost, high levels of subsidies to households, and farmers the power sector is incurring losses. The World Bank (2003 C) estimates that an average household pay 60% of the cost of supply, farmers pay 10%. In Karnataka households were currently estimated to consume 14% of total supply and farmers about 28%. The Planning Commission estimates that the implicit subsidy to agricultural consumers grew fourfold from 1992–1993 to Rs. 305 billion in 2001–2002 (1.3% of GDP) while that to households grew six fold. In short Indian farmers get very cheap power. It is felt that it is the better off section of society who benefit more by these subsidies.

EXPENDITURE REFORMS TO SUPPORT TO PUBLIC ENTERPRISES

The state governments have aimed at closing and privatizing loss making public enterprises but it will not give gains immediately. The details pertaining to the reforms by states in public enterprises is given in Table 3.

Table 3
Statement Showing the Reforms in Public Sector Enterprises—2004

Sl. No.	*Name of the State*	*Approx No. of State level PES*	*PES identi-fied for reforms*	*PES which reform process initiated*	*PES Priva-tised*	*PES closed*	*PES Re-Struc-tured*
1.	Andhra Pradesh	128	87	79	13	12	6
2.	Bihar	54	6	6	0	0	0
3.	Gujarat	54	24	24	3	6	0
4.	Haryana	45	8	6	1	4	0
5.	Karnataka	85	39	20	2	11	0
6.	Kerala	111	55	40	0	10	0
7.	Madhya Pradesh	26	14	14	1	0	0
8.	Maharashtra	65	11	04	0	0	0
9.	Orissa	72	33	10	9	11	0
10.	Punjab	53	11	11	1	6	0
11.	Rajasthan	28	10	6	1	1	0
12.	Tamil Nadu	59	29	29	0	7	2
13.	Uttar Pradesh	41	25	25	1	14	1
14.	West Bengal	82	15	15	0	0	0
	Total 903	367	289	289	32	82	9

Source: www. divest.nic.in (2004).

Of the total of 903 state level public enterprises 82 (9.1%) are closed 32 (3.5%) are privatized. In 289 (32%) reforms were initiated and 9 (1%) restructured. Among the states, Andhra Pradesh is in the top in the initiation of reform process and privatization. West Bengal has not privatized nor closed or restructured though started reforms in 16 public enterprises.

CAPITAL EXPENDITURE

In the budget estimates for 2003–2004, capital expenditure is budgeted to rise by 41% as against 39.9% in the previous year. The capital outlay is budgeted to increase by 34% in 2003–04. Higher than 28.8% in 2002–03. This rise is mainly due to increase in expenditures to education, sports, art and culture (35.3%). Rural development (73.4%) and food storage and warehousing (16.2%). To discharge internal debt and repayment of loans to the center are budgeted to increase by 52.7% and 17.2 as against the growth of 36.2% and 61.5% respectively in 2002–2003. The loans and advances extended by states are estimated to decline by 14.5% in 2003–04 as against the growth rate of 46.4% in 2002–03.

The reforms in the capital expenditure are aimed at increase in expenditure on education, sports, art and culture, rural development and food storage, discharge of internal debt and repayment of loans to the center. However advances extended by states to decline.

REFORMS IN THE REVENUE RECEIPTS

State governments get broadly two types of revenue. One is tax revenue, the other one is non-tax revenue. Tax revenue has got two components, one is own tax revenue and other is share in the central taxes. Sameway non-tax revenue has got two components. One is own non-tax revenue and the other is grants from the center.

STATES OWN TAX REVENUE

The details pertaining to states own tax revenue is given in Table 4. The own tax revenue of the States which was constituted 42.5% in 1960–61 has increased to 49.8% in 2001–2002. Among the states the efforts made by Maharashtra (71.4%) Kerala (69.5%) Tamilnadu (68.7%) it is appreciable where as the effort made by Jammu Kashmir (12.6%), Bihar (22%) Assam (24.1%) Orissa (29.3%) did least effort in raising their own Tax Revenue. Though reforms have been introduced in the collection of Tax Revenue. In 2003–04 Bihar, Gujarath, Jammu Kashmir, Karnataka and Rajasthan, Tamilnadu, Tripura, Uttar Pradesh, exhibited high rate of growth in own Revenue Receipts.

Table 4
Ratio of State's own Tax Revenue to Total Revenue Receipts of the Concerned States

Sl. No.	State	1960–61	1970–71	1980–81	1990–91	2000–01	2001–02
1.	Andhra Pradesh	46.7	52.3	46.0	49.5	53.0	52.4
2.	Assam	36.7	28.4	12.6	23.6	20.7	24.1
3.	Bihar	39.6	37.0	28.0	36.4	25.8	22.0
4.	Gujarat	39.8	51.7	51.8	71.0	56.0	52.0
5.	Haryana	–	52.8	50.8	55.9	62.9	64.1
6.	Jammu Kashmir	9.4	13.1	14.6	14.1	11.6	12.6
7.	Karnataka	35.6	49.2	49.8	60.2	61.8	62.0
8.	Kerala	45.3	46.5	52.6	55.8	67.2	69.5
9.	Madhya Pradesh	39.5	39.0	34.0	38.6	40.4	41.9
10.	Maharashtra	55.7	59.3	55.5	58.9	68.6	71.4
11.	Orissa	25.2	27.8	21.3	30.8	30.9	29.3
12.	Punjab	39.0	56.3	61.4	65.4	50.1	52.0
13.	Rajasthan	38.8	38.9	30.6	33.2	42.8	46.8
14.	Tamil Nadu	42.3	52.9	49.9	61.4	68.3	68.7
15.	Uttar Pradesh	42.1	37.2	34.0	38.1	38.4	42.2
16.	West Bengal	57.2	50.4	47.1	51.9	41.8	47.3
17.	All states	42.5	45.3	40.6	45.7	48.2	49.8

Source: Computed from RBI CMIE Reports.

The States which exhibited some rate of growth in revenue receipts are Andhra Pradesh, Assam, Chattisgarh, Goa, Himachal Pradesh, Jammu & Kashmir, Madhya Pradesh, Maharashtra, Manipur, Meghalaya, Mizoram, Orissa, Punjab and Sikkim.

RATIO OF STATES TOTAL TAX REVENUE TO TOTAL REVENUE RECEIPTS

The details pertaining to this is given in Table 5. It is evident that the proportion of tax revenue to total revenue receipts in 2001-2002 is highest in Bihar (85.1) Kerala (84.9) Tamilnadu (84.9) and Uttar Pradesh (81.4) where as the share of tax revenue in the revenue receipts of the states in the year 2001-2003 is lowest in Jammu Kashmir (23.4) Assam (50.6) Punjab (58.4). Thus there is a need to increase the share of tax revenue in the total revenue receipts by Jammu and Kashmir.

Table 5
Ratio of State's Total Tax revenues to Total Revenue Receipts of the Concerned States

Sl. No.	State	1960–61	1970–71	1980–81	1990–91	2000–01	2001–02
1.	Andhra Pradesh	65.0	74.2	69.4	70.9	73.4	72.1
2.	Assam	51.5	46.5	31.4	51.1	46.3	50.6
3.	Bihar	59.8	76.4	70.9	63.8	83.5	85.1
4.	Gujarat	72.8	69.8	70.3	79.3	65.0	60.6
5.	Haryana	–	67.4	64.1	65.6	71.1	71.3
6.	Jammu Kashmir	21.1	26.0	25.8	42.1	22.3	23.4
7.	Karnataka	50.5	67.4	70.5	77.3	79.0	80.0
8.	Kerala	59.0	67.2	76.2	76.0	84.7	84.9
9.	Madhya Pradesh	56.8	64.4	60.7	62.6	69.4	69.9
10.	Maharashtra	69.3	77.9	72.0	70.2	77.8	80.0
11.	Orissa	43.7	53.3	48.7	62.8	67.0	69.1
12.	Punjab	52.3	68.2	75.9	77.9	57.2	58.4
13.	Rajasthan	55.2	61.3	53.8	54.1	65.4	72.4
14.	Tamil Nadu	58.7	73.3	72.7	81.1	84.1	84.9
15.	Uttar Pradesh	64.1	68.3	67.3	65.8	75.0	81.4
16.	West Bengal	70.4	74.9	75.5	77.3	69.6	77.5
17.	All states	60.5	67.7	63.9	67.1	69.0	71.1

Source: Computed from RBI CMIE Reports.

Table 6
Total Tax Revenues as a Percent of G.S.D.P. in 1994–95 & 2000–01

Sl. No.	State	1994–95	2000–01
1.	Andhra Pradesh	8.9	10.5
2.	Assam	8.3	10.6
3.	Bihar	17.8	19.3
4.	Gujarat	9.0	9.5
5.	Haryana	8.4	9.3
6.	Karnataka	11.3	11.2
7.	Kerala	11.4	10.5
8.	Madhya Pradesh	13.2	13.2
9.	Maharashtra	8.6	9.1
10.	Orissa	9.7	13.8
11.	Punjab	8.8	8.6
12.	Rajasthan	8.7	10.7
13.	Tamil Nadu	11.0	11.3
14.	Uttar Pradesh	9.4	11.4
15.	West Bengal	8.9	7.7

Source: Computed from RBI & CMIE Reports.

TOTAL TAXT REVENUE AS PERCENTAGE OF GSDP IN 1994–95 AND 2000–2001

It is evident from the data given in Table 6 that in the year 2000–2001 the performance of Bihar (19.30) Orissa (13.8) Madhya Pradesh (13.2) is appreciable whereas the performance of developed states is poor. For example it is 7.7 for West Bengal 8.6 for Punjab 9.1 for Maharashtra 9.3 for Haryana and 9.5 for Gujarat. It is evident form the data given in the above table that poor states are collecting more revenue from their GSDP than developed states.

SHARE IN CENTRAL TAXES AS A PROPORTION OF TOTAL REVENUE RECEIPTS OF CONCERNED STATES IN PER CENT

As per Table 7 all the states together receive 21.3% of central taxes as proportion of their total revenue receipts in the year 2001–2002. Where as the same was 18% in the year 1960–61. It was highest in the year 1980–81 when it was 23.3%. Among the states whose position increased during the period 1960–61 to 2001–02 are Andhra Pradesh, Assam, Bihar, Karnataka, Kerala, Madhya Pradesh, Orissa, Rajasthan, Uttar Pradesh and West Bengal who have received more in 2001–02 in comparison with 1960–61. The states whose position is worsened are Haryana, Gujarat, Jammu Kashmir, Maharashtra, Punjab.

The highest beneficiary of the share in Central taxes in the year 2001–02 are Bihar (67.1%) Orissa (39.8%) Uttar Pradesh (39.2%). The states of Haryana, Punjab, Gujarat and Maharashtra have received lower share in the Central Taxes.

BUOYANCE OF STATES TAXATION

It is felt that own tax revenues of the state governments are not buoyant. This is because many states are following the traditional tax system. Though some states have appointed taxation enquiry committees but the governments are afraid of vote bank. Therefore though GSDP and NSDP have increased but Tax Revenues have not increased in many states. Therefore the Tax Revenues are not Buoyant. The details of this is given in Table 8.

Table 7
Ratio of Central Taxes as a Proportion of Total Revenue Receipts of the Concerned States

(Per cent)

Sl. No.	*State*	*1960–61*	*1970–71*	*1980–81*	*1990–91*	*2000–01*	*2001–02*
1.	Andhra Pradesh	18.2	21.9	23.4	20.4	20.8	19.7
2.	Assam	14.8	18.1	18.8	27.4	25.6	26.5
3.	Bihar	20.2	39.4	42.9	37.4	57.7	63.1
4.	Gujarat	32.9	18.1	18.5	8.3	9.1	8.6
5.	Haryana	–	14.6	13.3	9.7	8.1	3.2
6.	Jammu & Kashmir	11.7	12.9	11.2	28.0	10.7	10.8
7.	Karnataka	15.0	18.2	20.7	17.1	17.2	18.0
8.	Kerala	13.7	20.7	23.6	20.2	17.5	15.4
9.	Madhya Pradesh	17.5	25.4	26.7	24.0	29.0	28.0
10.	Maharashtra	13.6	18.6	16.5	11.4	9.2	8.6
11.	Orissa	18.4	25.5	27.4	32.0	36.1	39.8
12.	Punjab	13.3	11.9	14.5	12.6	7.1	6.4
13.	Rajasthan	16.4	22.4	23.4	20.8	22.7	25.6
14.	Tamil Nadu	16.4	20.4	22.8	19.7	15.8	16.2
15.	Uttar Pradesh	22.0	31.1	33.3	27.7	36.6	39.2
16.	West Bengal	19.2	24.5	28.4	25.4	27.8	30.2
17.	All states	18.0	22.4	23.3	21.4	20.8	21.3

Source: Computed from RBI CMIE Reports.

It is evident from the data in the above table that the Buoyancy of the own tax revenue is almost is around 80% for states like Karnataka, Kerala, Maharashtra and Tamilnadu, it is 0.8%. For Jammu Kashmir which is lowest (0.77).

In comparison with 1960–61 to 2001–02 the buoyancy has come down from 1.23 to 0.83 for Bihar, 1.03 to 0.82 Gujarat, 1.44 to 0.85 Jammu & Kashmir, 1.44 to 0.77 for Karnataka from 1.37 to 0.85 for Kerala 1.11 to 0.85 for Madhya Pradesh 1.17 to 0.83 for Maharashtra 1.49 to 0.85 for Orissa from 1.14 to 0.80 for Tamilnadu 1.64 to 0.85. However during the same period the states whose own tax revenue Buoyancy increased are Assam (0.01 to 0.78) Haryana (0.71 to 0.83) Punjab (0.03 to 0.83). In short the buoyancy of own tax revenue for the states has not increased as percentage of GSDP.

Therefore there is a need to initiate tax reforms at the state level. In order to strengthen their finances, states have initiated measures towards enhancement/rationaliza tion of various taxes such as land revenue, motor vehicle taxation, entertainment tax, sales tax, electricity duty, professional tax, entry tax, stamps and registration.

Table 8
State wise Buoyancy Rates for States own Tax Revenue for 1960–61 to 2001–02

Sl. No	*State*	*1960–61 to 1970–71*	*1970–71 to 1980–81*	*1980–81 to 1990–91*	*1990–91 to 1995–96*	*1995–96 to 2001–02*	*1990–91 to 2001–02*
1.	Andhra Pradesh	1.23	1.52	1.12	0.52	0.83	0.83
2.	Assam	0.01	1.03	1.33	0.78	0.78	0.78
3.	Bihar	1.03	1.22	1.07	–0.74	0.83	0.82
4.	Gujarat	1.44	1.28	1.19	0.77	0.85	0.85
5.	Haryana	0.71	1.37	1.10	0.87	0.83	0.83
6.	Jammu & Kashmir	1.44	1.25	1.30	0.58	0.77	0.77
7.	Karnataka	1.37	1.39	1.20	0.89	0.85	0.85
8.	Kerala	1.11	1.54	1.25	0.83	0.85	0.85
9.	Madhya Pradesh	1.17	1.36	1.13	1.36	0.84	0.83
10.	Maharashtra	1.49	1.13	1.09	0.83	0.85	0.85
11.	Orissa	1.14	1.30	1.41	0.60	0.80	0.80
12.	Punjab	0.03	1.21	1.00	1.08	0.83	0.83
13.	Rajasthan	1.10	1.37	1.12	0.85	0.82	0.82
14.	Tamil Nadu	1.64	1.20	1.04	0.81	0.85	0.85
15.	Uttar Pradesh	1.04	1.40	1.19	0.87	0.83	0.82
16.	West Bengal	1.08	1.31	1.24	0.88	0.81	0.82
17.	All states	1.22	1.28	1.13	0.89	0.85	0.85

Source: Computed from RBI CMIE Reports.

Due to reduction in sales tax to attract investment has led to revenue losses. States have decided to go for VAT in place of commercial tax, which is in use in 120 countries is viewed as a historic reform. VAT is expected to increase revenue. Government is planning to levy service tax to increase revenues.

NON TAX REVENUE

States have taken up reforms in the non-tax revenues also with a view to increase revenues from their sources. Revision in the tuition fee, medical fee, irrigation water rates, taxation on Urban Water supply etc.

The growth rate in non tax revenue in central government is budgeted decline while states own non tax revenue would be higher in 2003–04. This increasing reliance on states own non tax revenue will be expected to lead to fiscal consolidation.

If we consider buoyancy rates for states non tax revenue during the period i.e., 1960–61 to 2001–02 the data which is given in the Table 9.

Table 9
State wise Buoyancy Rates for Total non Tax Revenue For 1960–61 to 2001–02

Sl. No	*State*	*1960–61 to 1970–71*	*1970–71 to 1980–81*	*1980–81 to 1990–91*	*1990–91 to 1995–96*	*1995–96 to 2001–02*	*1990–91 to 2001–02*
1.	Andhra Pradesh	0.89	1.63	1.03	0.77	0.80	0.80
2.	Assam	0.03	1.41	1.10	0.91	0.84	0.84
3.	Bihar	0.77	1.64	1.44	–0.41	0.83	0.83
4.	Gujarat	1.20	1.11	0.97	0.89	0.79	0.79
5.	Haryana	0.68	1.43	1.07	2.37	0.82	0.82
6.	Jammu & Kashmir	1.23	1.10	1.28	1.19	0.91	0.91
7.	Karnataka	1.05	1.22	0.87	0.77	0.78	0.79
8.	Kerala	1.07	1.17	0.81	0.58	0.76	0.77
9.	Madhya Pradesh	1.12	1.42	0.97	1.16	0.82	0.82
10.	Maharashtra	1.20	1.24	1.09	0.58	0.78	0.79
11.	Orissa	0.96	1.60	0.86	0.72	0.81	0.81
12.	Punjab	–0.01	1.07	0.85	1.73	0.81	0.80
13.	Rajasthan	1.22	1.69	1.08	0.84	0.81	0.82
14.	Tamil Nadu	1.16	1.13	0.90	0.36	0.76	0.77
15.	Uttar Pradesh	1.11	1.42	1.08	0.75	0.79	0.80
16.	West Bengal	1.09	1.07	1.08	0.44	0.75	0.76
17.	All states	1.07	1.43	1.04	0.83	0.83	0.83

Source: Computed from RBI CMIE Reports.

Show that Buoyancy rates for all the states are not uniform in 1960–61 to 1970–71. It is 1.07 to all India i.e., all states. It is highest to Jammu Kashmir (1.23), Rajasthan (1.22) Gujarat (1.20). It was very low to Punjab (0.01) Assam (0.03) haryana (0.68). It is clear that buoyancy rates were higher to poor states than developed states. If we consider it for the period 1990–91 to 2001–02 the buoyancy rates of total non-tax revenue has decreased (instead of increasing). From all states together it is 0.83. It is highest for Jammu & Kashmir (0.91) and lowest for West Bengal 90.76).

The above data suggest that reforms are necessary to increase total non tax revenue in the states keeping in view the poor people and by following differential rates, this is the important agenda for state level fiscal reforms.

STATEWISE COMPARISON OF GROWTH RATES FOR GRANTS IN AID FROM CENTRE FOR DIFFERENT PERIODS

The compound growth rates of grants in aid from center to states remained almost stagnant during the period 1960–61 to 1980–83 (14.76) and 1960–61 to 2001–2002 (14.87). However it was highest at (18.88) during the period 1983–84 to 1988–89. These were slightly lower at 18.62% during the period 1989–90 to 1994–95. However the 12th Finance Commission suggested linking the grants in aid with economic reforms. It has suggested to provide Rs. 1,42,640 crores to the states in the form of grants during the period 2005 to 2010. This is 143.5% more when compared to 11th Finance Commission recommendations. The 12th Finance Commission also suggested to increase tax DGP ratio to 17.6% as well as to bring down revenue deficit of state and central governments to zero by the year 2008–2009. It has also suggested to bring down interest payments as a percentage to revenue receipts at the center to the 28% and at the states 15%.

The share of grants in the Non-Tax Revenue compound growth rate is highest to Haryana in the period 1960–61 to 1982–83 and it was lowest to Assam (10.77) and Tamilnadu (10.78) when we take into consideration compound growth rate of grants in aid during the 40 year period i.e., 1960—61 to 2001–2002. It was highest to Haryana (27.9) and is lowest to Kerala (12.03). If the states introduce reforms in the non-tax revenue the states need not depend on center for grants. The details of the above discussion are given in Table 10.

REFORMS IN THE PUBLIC DEBT OF THE STATE GOVERNMENTS

It is the states that determine the demand for debt, it is the center that controls the supply. How the central government regulates the state debt has an important bearing on fiscal sustainability at the state level. The states have six sources for financing the deficits which are subject to central control— these are (1) Govt. of India (Central Plan) loans. (2) Market Borrowing (3) Negotiated loans (4) Small Savings (5) Provident Funds (6) Other Public Accounts.

Table 10
State wiseCompund Growth Rates for Grants-In-Aid From Centre for Different Periods

Sl. No	*State*	*1960–61 to 1982–83*	*1983–84 to 1988–89*	*1988–89 to 1994–95*	*1995–96 to 2001–02*	*1960–61 to 2001–02*
1.	AndhraPradesh	14.05	13.65	19.46	10.34	14.12
2.	Assam	10.77	22.07	21.66	–5.34	13.77
3.	Bihar	14.42	16.71	21.56	–4.37	13.59
4.	Gujarat	13.32	24.35	27.31	38.98	14.25
5.	Haryana (66–67 to 00–01)	59.45	21.27	17.70	25.90	27.90
6.	Jammu Kashmir	16.55	15.19	33.05	–14.35	16.62
7.	Karnataka	8.56	15.91	22.26	18.14	12.92
8.	Kerala	10.95	9.95	23.30	8.57	12.03
9.	Madhya Pradesh	12.96	20.62	19.92	8.01	14.63
10.	Maharashtra	12.97	17.60	13.17	19.13	14.71
11.	Orissa	14.61	18.95	12.97	5.79	12.59
12.	Punjab	9.34	19.40	19.72	45.11	12.67
13.	Rajasthan	15.62	33.10	21.59	8.89	14.71
14.	Tamil Nadu	10.78	12.72	16.79	11.08	13.70
15.	Uttar Pradesh	15.68	12.66	17.77	3.52	14.79
16.	West Bengal	13.54	32.64	19.52	11.20	13.81
17.	All states	14.76	18.88	18.62	11.40	14.87

Source: Computed from RBI CMIE Reports.

However the borrowing capacity of the states depends upon Central Govt. control. Debt-NSDP Ratio of States for 2001–2002 is given below;

Below 30%: Under this category Karnataka, Maharashtra and Tamilnadu comes. These states have lesser debt burden.

Between 30 and 40%: Andhra Pradesh, Goa, Gujarat, Haryana, Kerala, Madhya Pradesh, Chattisgarh and Meghalaya states comes under this category.

Between 40 and 50%: Rajasthan, Uttar Pradesh, Uttaranchal, West Bengal, Assam and Tripura comes under this category.

Above 50%: Under this category the states such as Bihar, Jharkhand, Orissa, Punjab, Arunachal Pradesh, Himachal Pradesh, Manipur, Mizoram, Sikkim comes under this category. These states are having the highest debt burden among the Indian states.

The major deficit indicators is given in Table 11 as percentage of GDP.

Table 11
Statement Showing the Major Deficit Indicators of State Governments

Sl. No.	*Type of deficit*	*2003–04 BE*	*2002–03 RE*	*2002–03 BE*	*2001–02 Actuals*	*2000–01 Actuals*
1.	GFD	4.2	4.7	4.0	4.2	4.3
2.	RD	1.8	2.5	1.9	2.6	2.6
3.	PD	1.2	1.7	1.2	1.5	1.8

Source: State Fiances—A study of budgets of 2002–04; RBI April, 2004.

The gross fiscal deficit which was 4.3 in 2000–2001 is estimated to be 4.2 in 2003–04. The revenue deficit is also estimated to come down from 2.6 in 2000–2001 to 1.8. During the same period the primary deficit is expected to come down from 1.8 to 1.2.

POWER SECTOR REFORMS

With a view to reduce losses in the power sector and government allocations, several states initiated power sector reforms. The state electricity boards (SEBs) account for the bulk of the states investment in SEBs and poor financial performance of SEBs led to fiscal crisis at the states level Power sector reforms include Constitution of States Electricity Regulatory Commission (SERCs) for determining tariff structure, Unbundering of electricity boards into separate entity for power generation, transmission and distribution increasing power tariffs as well as measures for reducing transmission and distribution losses.

Twenty one states have constituted Electricity Regulatory Commission for determining the power tariff structure. Of these 21 states, 17 states have become operational, 16 states have issued tariff orders. Based on the recommendations of the Ahluwalia Committee 2001 Scheme for one time settlement of outstanding dues to the State Electricity Boards to CPSUs was finished. Tripartite Agreements have been signed among the government of India, the RBI and 28 state governments. Under the scheme the state governments have issued 15 years bonds during 2003–04 w.e.f., 1.10.2001 worth Rs. 28984 crores to the CPSUs in exchange of the outstanding dues at a nominal tax free interest rate of 8.5% per annum, repayable over 10 years after a moratorium period of 5 years. 10% of the bonds can be offered in the market every year for trading.

The Govt. of India also initiated measures to encourage fiscal reforms at the states level. The XI Finance Commission earmarked incentive fund with a corpus of Rs. 10,607 crore over a period of 5 years for encouraging fiscal reforms at the states level.

The Planning Commission is also extending support to the reforms. Reforms Programme is approved for 23 states. MOU is signed with 16 states and Rs. 3722 crore have been released. Govt. of India shares the cost of reforms in the states such as voluntary retirement scheme downsizing of PSUs. The center contribute finance 80% of such costs for special category states and 60% to non special category states.

Recommending the need for reducing the interest burden of the states allocating from the center to the states bearing coupons in excess of 13% are to be swapped with market borrowings and small savings proceeds at prevailing interest rates over a period of three years ending in 2004–05.

Reserve Bank of India also provides incentives to the state governments to undertake fiscal reforms at the state level. The 12th Finance Commission also provides incentives for those states which undertake state level fiscal reforms.

The state of Andhra Pradesh is in the first place among the Indian states in implementing state level fiscal reforms in 1996–97. Prohibition was partially rolled back. Issue price of subsidized rice was raised to Rs. 3.50 per kg. Fresh recruitment has been stopped. Large public enterprises such as Hyderabad Allwyn was privatized. In 1997–1998 irrigation rates were raised by five times. Water user associations were formed. Women and poor were organized under DWCRA. Joint Forest Management and Watershed Management was initiated. In the year 1998–99 participation of the people was extended to cover the management of village schools, hospitals etc. Power Tariff was hiked by 9%. E-Governance has been introduced, Foreign direct investment and NRI investments have been encouraged. Indian School of Business, Indian Institute of Information Technology were established. To achieve long-term reforms Vision 2020 was prepared. In 1990–2000 tax based incentives to industries was withdrawn. User charges have been hiked in Road Transport Corporation, Municipal Corporation etc. Fiscal reforms were sought to be used as instrument of growth.

Gross interest payments have been reduced from 20.9% in 2001–02 to 11.8% in 2003–04. Development expenditure has been increased from 2.9% in 2001–02 to 8.5% in 2003–04. Non-development expenditure is decreased from 16.1% to 10.7% during the same period. The plan expenditure is increased from 1.9% in 2001–02 to 12.4% in 2002–03. Non-plan expenditure is decreased from 10.6% to 9.7% during the same period. Non-plan Non-development expenditure is also decreased from 16.1% to 10.9%.

In short it is evident that the public expenditure in the states is decreasing on non-priority unproductive activities and increasing in favour of productive and priority activities.

However the peoples opinion is against these reforms. When electricity rates were increased, RTC fares were increased, water charges increased and user charges increased the political parties and people agitated for this and defeated the parties in power in the general elections during 2003 and 2004.

A RESUME

The aim of fiscal reforms at the state level is to improve the fiscal health of the state governments. The reforms of liberalization, privatization and globalization are based on the classical theory of economics. The classical theory is based on the assumption of existence of full employment and ideal situation. Because of the fiscal ill health for the last several years for several countries forced such Nations and sub-national regions forced to go for the help from the International Institutions such as IMF, IBRD and ADB as well as International Financial markets which are dominated by economic giants. Such as USA, UK, France, Australia, Germany etc., They were facing the crisis of depression as they were producing more than they were consuming which resulted excess of supply over demand which led for the increased unemployment, lower rate of investment and lower growth of the economy. These giants wanted opportunities for their investments and markets for their goods and they wanted to influence the particularly the third world countries to liberalise and globalise those economies. So that these economic giants can activate their economic activity by exporting their goods and their money. Therefore they have suggested economic reforms in countries such as India. Since these countries were in need of foreign investment to cure their economies. They accepted the conditions put forth by them. The reforms are successful only in few countries such as China but they are not successful in many countries which made such countries to depend more and more on economic super powers.

We are not against economic reforms both at National and Sub National levels but they must help to improve the health of the economies. Fiscal reforms are part of the economic reforms. In a federation like India reforms at the central level makes states also to undertake reforms at the state level. In view of this states have initiated several reforms including fiscal reforms. Therefore there is a need for agenda of fiscal and other reforms at the state level, which are summarized herein below:

1. To increase the plan-expenditure
2. To increase the capital expenditure
3. To increase the development expenditure
4. To increase the Revenue Receipts

By undertaking appropriate policies towards raising tax revenue by undertaking reforms in the state taxation as well as reforms in the non-tax revenue. There are several avenues for the state governments to increase their tax revenues by undertaking agricultural income tax which has to be imposed on very large, large and medium farmers. Sales Tax can also be increased on the luxury and semi luxury items. Excise duty has to be increased on several products of well to do consumption goods. Particularly on liquors, cars, other motor vehicles. Entertainment tax has to be increased.

So far as Non-Tax Revenues are concerned, there is a scope to increase energy charges, water charges, transport charges, irrigation charges, medical and health charges etc., when this measure is undertaken poor people should be kept in mind.

There is a need and scope for the reduction in the subsidies. At present in many states power is provided to the farmers at the nominal rates. Therefore power to be supplied at free of cost only to the marginal and small farmers and reasonable charges have to be collected from large farmers same way irrigation charges particularly under canal irrigation have to be increased several times. Fertilizers subsidy to be withdrawn and encourage compost manure use. This will not only reduce the cost of subsidy to government but also saves the fertility of the land and health of the people. Many of the industries are provided water and power at subsidized rates. Therefore there is need to classify the industries as priority and non-priority industries. These subsidies are to be provided only to priority industries.

REFORMS IN THE PUBLIC SECTOR UNDERTAKINGS:

The first Prime Minister of the country late Pandit Jawaharlal Nehru stated that starting of industries in the public sector will pave the way for social justice. He felt that profits earned in the public sector undertakings will be ploughed back. Thus investment will increase, employment will increase, incomes will increase, standard of living will increase and poverty will be reduced. But of late it is found that due to several reasons including political leaders interference and trade union activities, public sector has become a loss making entity. Therefore government felt to privatize them. However the voluntary retirement scheme, dis-investment scheme were not successful. Government even planned to privatize the profit making PSUs also for which there is opposition from its employees and left parties. Therefore it is suggested all the priority industries such as steel mills, machine tools, chemical industries, power sector must be in the public sector only. No FDI is to be allowed in these sectors. Thus it will become strong foundation for economic development.

REFORMS IN THE BORROWING

Today the state governments are approaching World Bank and other International Financial Institutions for loans. Even for the construction of roads, flyovers irrigation projects etc., foreign loans are obtained. Repayment of these loans will not only become burdensome but also costly.

Therefore, it is suggested that internal borrowing to be resorted which will not be burdensome. It will represent only transfer of resources from people to the government. When these loans are re-paid the resources will be transferred from government to the people. The Reserve Bank also increase the money supply (or resort to deficit finance) and provide loans to the state governments. The traditional economists argue that deficit finance or increase in money supply will lead to inflation which is not correct. Where do we get money (i.e., from World Bank or Reserve bank or through Market Borrowings or from Central Government) is not important where do we put the money is important or what do we do with the money (are we investing in the long gestation projects i.e., steel mills, railways, hydro electric projects or irrigation projects which are inflationary in nature or are we investing in short gestation projects such as minor irrigation tanks, tube wells, dug wells, small scale industries which are not only short gestation activities but also inflation dampening activities) which is important. So far as there exists balanced allocation ratio between long gestation projects (inflation creating activities), and short gestation projects (inflation dampening activities) there prevails non-inflationary balanced growth. Even payment of rate of interest is also not burdensome. Because it is the tax payers who receive interest payments and both will cancel out each other.

Without any loss of efficiency by introducing reforms in the administration lot of unproductive non-development expenditure can be saved, for this purpose the number of ministers, security personnel for ministers, chairman for the corporations, IAS, IPS and other posts have to be reduced. Even it is suggested to close the legislative councils.

CONCLUSION

If the above fiscal and other reforms are implemented we can achieve debt free, inflation free sustainable development in the country.

REFERENCES

State Fiscal Reforms in India: Progress & Prospects—A World Bank Report Published by Macmillan India Ltd., 2005 New Delhi.

State Finances: A study of budgets of 2003–04 published by Reserve bank of India, Mumbai, April 2004.

Growth of Tax Revenues in Andhra Pradesh (1960–61) to 2001-2002 published by Directorate of Economics and Statistics, Govt. of Andhra Pradesh, Hyderabad Feb. 2003.

Economic Survey 2003–2004 Govt. of India Ministry of Finance Economic Division, New Delhi.

Statistical Outline of India 2003–04, Tata Services Ltd., Dept. of Economics and Statistics, Bombay House, Mumbai Jan. 2004.

Economy of Maharashtra Problems and Prospects, edited by Dr. V.B. Jugale and Dr. A.A. Dange, Shivaji University, Kolhapur, Dept. of Economics, Dec. 2003.

Economy of Uttar Pradesh–Emerging Challenges edited by Dr. Mad.huri Srivastava, Banaras Hindu University, Dept. of Economics, Dee. 2004. Article of Dr. M. Narasimhulu on Finances of Uttar Pradesh State Government p. 98 to 111 Dec. 2004.

Dr. M. Narsimhulu "State Level Fiscal Reforms—A case study of Andhra Pradesh" published in Review of Politics, Volume XI Number 1 and 2 Jan–June and July-December 2003, Dept. of Political Science, Veer Kanwar Singh University Ara Bihar, June, 2003.

12th Finance Commission Report submitted to Parliament on 26th February, 2005.

Annual Fiscal Framework 2005–06, Government of Andhra Pradesh Finance Department, February, 2005.

V.M. Dandekan–Gross Domestic Product and Regional Disparities in Development in India. Published in Journal of Indian School of Political Economy XII 1 Jan-mar. 2003 p. 35–69.

B.P.R. Vittal "Government as Employer: its role, limitations and implications, Economic and Political Weekly" Vol. XIV 34, 25.8.1979.

B.P.R. Vittal and "Governments Salary Bill Rationale and Rationalisation" Published in Asian Economic Seminar August, 2002, 44, 1.

Holley Ulbrich "Public Finance in Theory and Practice' Clemson University published by Southern Western, Ohio USA 2003.

M. Narasimhulu "Fiscal Policy for Planned Development' Indian Journal of Public Administration Vol. XVIII No.3 July-Sept 1972.

M. Narasimhulu "Economic Reforms Prospect and Retrospect" published by Anmol Publications Pvt. Ltd., new Delhi in the Book.

Economic Development and the Ninth Five year Plan edited by V.B. Bhinse 1998.

M. Narasimhulu and B. Sudhakar Reddy "The overall planned development strategies in India and China with special reference to FDI' in the Book "A comparative study of foreign direct investment in China and India" edited by B. Satyanarayan, Published by Himalaya Publishing House, 1996, Delhi.

M. Narasimhulu and Mohd. Irfanullakhan, "Poverty and Sutainable Development an intra and inter regional analysis" published in the book "Poverty and Sustainable Development in Third World Perspectives" edited by Ravishankar Kumar Singh, published by Abhijit Publications, Delhi, 2005.

M. Narasimhulu "Indian Development Experience with a focus on inter-state disparities Cind the role of central transfers to reduce them" published in the book "Development Experience in the Indian Economy inter-state perspectives" edited by P.R. Brahmananda and V.R. Panchamukhi in Book Well, Delhi, 2001.

M. Narasimhulu and K. Vijaya Lakshmi "Management of Government Finances in India in the context of Economic Reforms" printed in the book "Economic Reforms in India" edited by Ravlshank Ravishankar Kumar Singh published by Abhijit Publications, Delhi, 2004.

15

REVIEW OF STATE GOVERNMENT FINANCES

A.A. Dange

INTRODUCTION

The Tenth Five Year Plan (2002–03 to 2006–07) aims at a growth rate of 8 per cent and also lays emphasis on poverty reduction, creation of more employment potential and higher infrastructure development both social and economic. Size of national investment is stipulated to rise from Rs. 2,507 Thousand Crore during the Ninth Plan to Rs. 4,082 Thousand Crore during the Tenth Plan period at constant 2001–02 prices (a increase of 62 per cent). For this to happen, investments in the economy will have to increase at an annual growth rate of 14 per cent. This is a challenging task since the long-run growth rate of investment in India has averaged around 6.5 per cent per annum. Average investment requirement for the Tenth Plan is 28.4 per cent of GDP for which domestic rate of savings have to increase as well as there has to be rise in public sector investment along with increase in private sector investment.

Attainment of the projected growth rate of such high magnitude necessarily needs an equally high level of public sector investment comprising both Central and State Government Public Sector Undertakings. Public sector investment trends in recent years reveal a declining trend and are about 7.2 per cent of GDP and this declining trend has to be reversed and increased to reach nearly

9.9 per cent of GDP. This is a challenging task. For the success of the Tenth Plan growth rate realization therefore the magnitude of public sector investment assumes significance. The macro economic impact of these investments would depend on the structural pattern of public investment, the extent of capacity utilization created through such investment, and most importantly the reaction of the private sector to the fiscal position of the government more so State Governments in terms of its expenditure management and revenue creation effort. It is in this context that fiscal consolidation at the sub-national level in India is crucial. Fiscal reforms at State level are important for today States raise about 37 per cent of total central and state revenues and account for about 60 per cent of total revenue expenditure. Of the combined revenue deficits of Centre and States-share of States is higher and their share in total fiscal deficit is also increasing. Therefore any successful attempt at undertaking fiscal consolidation measures to reduce fiscal and revenue deficits-reform of state level budgetary policies is vital.

It also has to be borne in mind that different components of public expenditure have very different multiplier effects on the rest of the economy. The strongest effect is through public investment and the weakest through subsidies and transfers. It is therefore very vital that revival of capital expenditure especially capital outlays have to take place in the expenditure pattern of states and this will necessitate expenditure management strategy that aims at revenue expenditure compression without reducing expenditure on social safety net. In stepping up the level of public investment, it is necessary to take into account also the role of public investment and public borrowings in a mixed economy like India. On the one hand, efforts to increase public investment through enhanced borrowings tend to reduce the private investment by pre-empting investible funds and causing what is known as 'crowding out'. On the other hand, private investment can be positively influenced by public investment-through demand-generating role and through creation of infrastructure. Rising fiscal deficits more so revenue deficits implies more reliance on borrowings by the States to finance their revenue expenditures and such trend in State finances are detrimental to the process of economic reforms. In addition increase in State Government guarantees also is increasing the aggregate debt liabilities of the State Governments in India and such a trend in rise in contingent liabilities can have an adverse impact on sovereign credit worthiness. It is against the above overall macro economic background that a review of State Finances assumes significance.

REVIEW OF STATE FINANCES

As set forth in the Indian Constitution, State Governments in India have important functions and responsibilities to perform in various economic and social sectors. They also have access to substantial revenue flow, including both own taxes and share in central taxes. In addition fiscal transfers from the central government also augment States; own revenues. Since 1980s however various fiscal problem are emerging in State finances. Public finance in India in the late 1990s and early 2000 has seen a rapid growth of revenue expenditure as well as revenue deficit both at Central and State level. Deficit growth on the revenue account is a trend seen in State finances from the late 1980s only prior to which States had a revenue account surplus. Growth in revenue account deficits represents unsound public finance as current expenditure financed through borrowings is unsustainable. When government borrowings are used to finance public investment outlays, one has no economic grounds to complain. On the other hand, when the fiscal deficit is increasingly used to finance revenue account expenditure it is unsound public finance practice. With emphasis on fiscal deficit reduction, States are facing budgetary squeeze. Though State Governments have succeeded in tax revenue mobilization, non tax revenue is not growing due to declining cost recovery rates for economic and social services provided by State governments and reluctance to do away with heavy subsidies. Public debt liabilities of the States have increased, leading to higher growth of interest liabilities which are a major cause for growth of revenue expenditure.

Rising revenue expenditure have reduced the State Government's ability to invest in capital outlays. In addition social sector spending which States in India do more than the Central government is also affected. Hence crisis in State finances have adverse repercussions on both economic growth and social welfare. In the last decade downward rigidity in committed State government expenditure along with fiscal stress has contributed to cutbacks on social service expenditures, which is vital for income distribution, reduction of regional disparities, employment generation and impact on the quality of life in terms of human capital formation and development. This has resulted in a situation of near stagnation in social expenditures at around 5.00 per cent of GDP during both 1980s and 1990s.

Overall Budgetary Position of State Governments

Table 1 adequately reveals that since 1991 onwards the State Government's revenue account deficits have increased more so after 1999–2000. This has resulted in more borrowed funds being used to finance current expenditure thus reducing the capital investment outlay of the States Gross fiscal deficits of States increased from 2.6 per cent of GDP in 1980–81 to 4.8 per cent of GDP by 1999–2000. However, borrowed funds were used to finance revenue account expenditure and not developmental outlays. Revenue account deficit of States in India as a ratio of GDP in recent years was 4.6 per cent in 1990–2000 and 4.3 per cent in 2000–2001(RE) and is estimated to be 3.8 per cent of GDP for the fiscal year 2001–2002 (BE). Latest budgetary estimates by the RBI for the current fiscal year reveal that States are aiming at to reduce the deficit levels. However, the methods envisage involve a deterioration in the quality of expenditure. In the current fiscal year (2001–2002) the combined fiscal deficit the States is budgeted to fall to 3.8 per cent of GDP from 4.3 per cent in 2000–2001. But this would be achieved through a relative fall in developmental expenditure to 9.3 per cent of GDP from 10.2 per cent last year. Non developmental expenditure however is set to increase from 5.6 per cent or 5.8 per cent of GDP. Hence the quality of fiscal adjustment of States become crucial all the more so because out of the total (Centre plus States) developmental expenditure, State government's share is over three fourth (2000–2001) within which 85 per cent is social sector expenditure.

Table 1
Overall Budgetary Position of State Governments in India

Rs. In Crores

Year	*REV/ACCTT Surplus (+) Deficit (–)*	*CAP ACCTT +/–*	*Overall (+/–)*	*Gross Fiscal Deficit*
1980–81	1486	–2383	–897	3713 (2.6)
1985–86	654	1034	1688	75.21 (2.7)
1990–91	–5309	5381	72	18787 (3.3)
1995–96	– 8201	11050	2849	31426 (2.6)
1999–00	–56801	47589	–9212	93739 (4.8)
2000–01	–45702	41400	–4302	90092 (4.1)
2001–02	–59188	55762	–3426	95994 (4.2)
2002–03 (RE)	–61240	56060	–5190	116636 (4.7)

Source: State Finance, A Study of Budgets 2003–04.

Table 2
Selected Fiscal Ratios State Governments

(Per cent)

Year	*Capital Outlay/ GFD*	*Interest payments/ Revenue Exp.*	*RD/GFD*
1985–90	62.4	10.8	7.7
1990–95	55.3	13.6	24.6
1995–2000	47.5	15.8	35.8
2002–2003 (RE)	35.6	20.9	52.5

Source: RBI, State Finances, December, 2000, State Finances: A Study of Budgets - 2003–04, page S23.

Trends in State Level Expenditure Pattern

Deterioration in the deficit level at the State level in the 1990s cannot be attributed to tax receipts as the State's tax revenue/GDP ratio has remained around 5.5 per cent in the last decade. Interest payments and other non interest, non developmental revenue expenditure are the main cause. Interest payments as per centage of revenue receipt have risen from 16.5 per cent in 1990–91 to 22 per cent in 2001–02, while administrative cost of running the government rose to 27 per cent of revenue receipts in 2001–02 from about 23 per cent in the last decade. In 2001–02 (BE) interest payments and the State government's non developmental revenue expenditure are budgeted to eat more than half of the revenue receipts. It is in this context that the quality of fiscal adjustment at the State level in India assumes significance as developmental and social sector expenditure reduction affects social welfare and the overall economic activity as well. Latest RBI Annual Report mentions that in the current year, the Centre and States will together spend just 2.8 per cent of GDP on education and the 1.3 per cent of GDP on health and family welfare levels which are comparably very low as far as Human development and Social Welfare is concerned.

Table 3
Trends in State Level Expenditure Pattern

Rs. In Crores

	1990–91	*1995–96*	*1999–2000 (RE)*	*2000–01 (BE)*	*2002–03 (RE)*
(i) Aggregate Disbursements	91242 (16.0)	177584 (14.9)	325634 (16.6)	350767 (16.1)	442641
(ii) Developmental Expenditure	63370 (11.1) (69.5)	114819 (9.7) (64.7)	198322 (10.1) (60.9)	208332 (9.6) (59.4)	247827
(iii) Non, Developmental Expenditure	22600 (4.0) (24.8)	55380 (4.7) (31.2)	110137 (5.6) (33.8)	125484 (5.8) (35.8)	160684
(iv) Plan Expenditure	27433 (4.8)	48450 (4.1)	78156 (4.0)	89074 (4.1)	105345
(v) Non Plan Expenditure	63809 (11.2) (69.9)	129134 (10.9) (72.7)	247478 (12.6) (76.0)	261693 (12.0) (74.6)	337297

Notes: (i) Figures in round brackets are % of GDP.
(ii) Figures in square brackets are % of Aggregate Disbursements.
Source: As of Table 1.

The above Table 5 reveals the pattern of State level expenditure in India. Data reveals that:

(i) State level developmental expenditure as per cent of GDP declined from 11.1 per cent in 1990–91 to 9.6 per cent in 2000–01. As a percentage of aggregate disbursements developmental expenditure shows decline from 69.5 per cent to 59.4 per cent in the last decade.

(ii) Share of non developmental expenditure in aggregate disbursements has risen from 24.8 per cent in 1990–91 to 35.8 per cent in 2000–01.

(iii) Plan expenditure of all States in India as per cent of GDP also shows declining trend from 4.8 per cent of GDP in 1990–91 to 4.1 per cent in 2000–01 (BE). Their share in aggregate disbursements also has declined Non plan expenditure of States as per cent of GDP rose from 11.2 per cent in 1990–91 to 12.0 per cent in 2000–01 (BE).

(iv) Of the total expenditure interest payments percentage share increased from 5.3 per cent in 1980–81 to 11.5 per cent in 1995–96 and further to 14 per cent in 1999–2000. As percentage of GDP interest payments and debt servicing of States in India rose from 0.9 per cent in 1980–85 to 2.2 per cent in 1995–96 and to 2.3 per cent in 1999–2000.

(v) As a per cent of GDP pension payments by States in India rose from 0.3 per cent of GDP in 1980–85 to 0.8 per cent in 1995–99 and to 0.9 per cent in 1999–2000.

(vi) Rapid increase in revenue account expenditure, revenue deficits have had adverse implication on the capital disbursements by States affecting vital capital developmental outlays. As a share of total expenditure capital disbursements by States declined from 31.3 per cent in 1980–85 to 20.0 per cent in 1990–95 and further down to 16.4 per cent in 1999–2000. Total capital outlays as percentage of total expenditure declined from 13.2 per cent in 1980–85 to 8.9 per cent in 1999–2000. As a percentage of GDP capital disbursements by States in India declined from 5.0 per cent in 198.85 to about 2.8 per cent in 1999–2000. Thus the trends in expenditure pattern at the State level in India reveals disturbing trends having adverse consequences on public investment in socio-economic infrastructure development as well as social sector spending.

Trends in the Revenue Pattern of State Governments in India

As depicted in the above table State revenue trends indicate that the States have succeeded in sustaining their own tax to GDP ratio during the 1990s in fact the ratio has increased. During the same period share in Central taxes as percentage of GDP has some what eroded from 2.5 per cent in 1990–91 to 2.3 per cent in 2000–01. It is to be noted that this has happened despite repeated increase in the States share in the divisible pool as recommended by the finance commission. Likewise grants from the Centre too have declined. Loans from the Centre have remained static at about 2.3 per cent of GDP Loans from the Centre to the States increased from Rs. 13974 crore in 1990–91 to Rs. 19600 crore in 1995–96 and further to Rs. 51893 crore by 2000–01 (BE), thus increasing the States' indebtedness to the Centre, subsequent to which repayment of loans to Centre increased from Rs. 3997 crore in 1990–91 to Rs. 4799 crore by 1995–96 and further to Rs. 9734 crore in 2000–01 thereby reducing the net Central loan availability to finance capital outlays. The trend in Central loans to States clearly reveals that Central financing of plan expenditure has no connection between viability of projects and their financing costs as the introduction of Gadgil formula for block plan assistance to States comprises of loans to the extent of 70 per cent regardless of the end use of the expenditures. There is no distinction between financing of public goods and semi-private goods, the consequences of which has resulted in low investment returns to the States.

FINANCING PATTERN OF STATE PLANS

In principle investment in public goods should result in higher tax revenues, whereas investment in private goods should result in higher revenues through the imposition of user changes for public services. Plan investment by States in India has gone more in financing of power generation, transmission and distribution of power through SEBS, financing of STRTC, financing urban infrastructure facilities, irrigation, housing etc. State public sector enterprises manage most of these whereas irrigation is administered directly by the government. Had these enterprises being able to impose appropriate pricing policies for services provided, they would have provided returns to State governments as dividends and would have been able to service their debt directly. Both have neither materialized and hence no net positive internal resources mobilized for financing expansion of services provided.

Table 4
Revenue Pattern of State Governments in India

(*Rs. in Crores*)

	1990–91	*1995–96*	*1999–2000*	*2002–03 (RE)*
(i) Total Revenue Receipts	66467 (11. 7)	136803 (11.5)	214810 (11.0)	294008
(ii) Tax Revenuer	44586 (7.8)	92913 (7.8)	150095 (7.7)	202502
(a) Own Tax Revebye	30345 (5.3)	63865 (5.4)	105637 (5.4)	145141
(b) Share in Central Taxes	14242 (25)	29048 (2.4)	44458 (2.3)	57361
(iii) Non Tax Revenue (I+II)	21881	43891	64714	91506
(a) Own Non Tax	9237 (1.6)	22896 (1.9)	29634 (1.5)	35956
(b) Grants from Centre	12643 (2.2)	20996 (1.8)	35081 (1.8)	55550
(iv) Total Capital Receipts	24847 (4.4)	43630 (3.7)	101612 (5.2)	143443
Of which Loans fom Centre	–13974 (2.5)	(19600) (1.6)	49527 (2.5)	30235
(v) Aggregate Revenue (I + IV)	91314	180433	316422	

Source: As of Table 1
Note: Figures in bracket are % of GDP.

Table 5 gives the details of the pattern of State plan financing. The contribution of balance from current revenues (BCR) to financing State plans which was as high as 40 per cent of the total VI FYP came down to 23 per cent in the VII FYP and has now declined to less than zero during the VIII FYP. Contributions of State PSEs has been consistently negative. Consequently the share of borrowings by State governments has increased substantially from about 37 per cent in VII FYP to 52 per cent in the VIII FYP and further envisaged to be higher in the IX FYP. Correspondingly share of Central assistance has also increased to more than 50 per cent by the VIII FYP signifying the growth of fiscal dependency of States on Central fiscal transfers. Situation in the IX FYP has turned still

Table 5
Financing Pattern of State plans

Source		*VIII FYP (1985–90) (Actual)*		*VIII FYP (1992–97)*		*IX FYP 1997–98*			
						Anti capated Outlay (Current Prices)		*1998–99 Approved Outlay (Current Prices)*	
		Rs. Crores	*Percent*	*Rs. Crores*	*Percent*	*Rs. Crores*	*Percent*	*Rs. Crores*	*Percent*
1.	Balance from Current Revenue	17368	23	–2009	–1.4	–87003	–17.7	–17360	–25
2.	Contribution of PESs	–3757	–5	–2723	–1.9		NA		NA
3.	Total Borrowings	27644	37	75750	52	38350	78	61110	88
4.	Total State Resources	41255	55	70335	48	29650	60	43750	63
5.	Central Assistance	33264	45	75750	52	19520	40	25695	37
6.	Total Resources	74519	100	146085	100	49172	100	69445	100

Source: (i) RBI, Report on Currency and Finance, Various Issues available on RBI. Website: www.rbi.org.in

bad with the BCR being negative meaning that borrowed funds are used to finance. Current revenue expenditure in substantial amount. Within borrowings share of market borrowings at higher interest rates is increasing in the last few years.

Financing of investments by States thus is becoming non sustainable. In addition there has been an increase of State government guarantees for their PSEs borrowings because of which the lending institutions are now beginning to question the quality of these q\guarantees. There is also a much greater demand by lenders that State governments subject themselves to credit ratings. The problem stated above hence needs immediate remedy. Expenditure on investment for the provision of private goods must be related more directly to the generation of returns through the levy of appropriate user charges. The problem at present is that because of the lack of correlation between borrowing ability and returns to the activity, the levy of user charges is essentially done politically. In addition for raising of resources for investments in provision of public goods the time has come to subject State governments systematically to credit ratings so that their ability to borrows depends on their fiscal health.

FUTURE COURSE OF ACTION

The present State of State finances is surely unsustainable and poses a grave threat to economic growth. Combined fiscal deficit of Centre and State stand today at 10 per cent of GDP. Half of borrowed funds are used to defray current expenditures resulting in decline in public sector investments at an alarming rate. As stated at the beginning sustaining higher growth needs to be done in the coming decade. This cannot be achieved unless a significant fiscal correction is successfully implemented. In addition poverty reduction needs enhanced social sector expenditure more so by States in India. Renewal of public investment in a wide variety of areas in social and economic infrastructure is essential for higher economic growth and poverty eradication.

Fiscal correlation and budget reform policies adopted by States in recent years as promulgated in the Budget speeches and other supplementary information provided by State Government reveals that policy initiatives proposed fall broadly into (a) Fiscal consolidation measure, (b) Institutional reforms and (c) Sectoral reforms. Moderation of expenditure, revenue augmentation, setting up of Expenditure Reform Committees, reduction in non-merit subsidies, fiscal restructuring through down sizing government, revenue augmentation through enhancement/restructuring of land revenue rates, vehicle tax, entertainment tax, sales tax, betting tax are the main fiscal consolidation measures adopted by States in the last few budgets. Implementation of harmonized floor rate of sales tax, as a prelude to introduction of uniform value added tax (VAT) is a major fiscal harmonization measure adopted.

Institutional reforms proposed in the State budgets aim at to strengthen fiscal consolidation. Improvement in governance and pursuit of decentralization, exploring ways to reduce cost of administration, freeze on fresh recruitment as well as reviewing man power requirement are major reforms undertaken. Establishment of Board of Financial and Managerial Restructuring by some States (Maharashtra, Karnataka) to undertake review of State PSEs, including possibility of close down of non-viable units, after providing suitable safety nets to employees, and VRS for employees are other institutional reforms adopted.

Sectoral reforms undertaken aim at to strengthen infrastructure sectors, commissioning of software technology parks to increase resource flow into IT sector are envisaged. Some States have proposed Export promotion Industrial Parks. In the agricultural sector reform initiatives include strengthening up horticulture, floriculture, waste land development, environment protection, development of wine parks etc. power sector reforms constitute yet another area of thrust in State budgets, States have outlined initiative aimed at restructuring the power sector through measures aimed at to private sector entry into power generation, reorganization of SEBs and establishment of independent regulatory/tariff authorities.

However, the key objective of fiscal reform in future has to be reduction in debt servicing payments. This can only be achieved by a progressive reduction in public debt and through higher tax and non tax revenue mobilization. Higher tax revenues can only to achieve through Buoyancy and expansion of the tax base and not through increase in tax rates. For this the following are suggested;

(i) Expansion of tax base

(ii) Wide spread and bold imposition of user charges on all non merit goods

(iii) Wide spread and bold privatization.

(iv) For higher tax revenues imposition of indirect tax on service sector is feasible and this can be achieved by a wide spread value added tax on all sectors of the economy. This would mean the levy of tax at every stage of value addition from production to sale of both goods and services. Levying such a tax will require necessary amendment to the constitution along with State Government consensus. Thus long term buoyancy in indirect tax revenue can be achieved by this structure change.

Absence of appropriate pricing policy of PSEs is a major cause for fiscal crisis. In case of power supply only lower than economic pricing to agriculture and domestic sector amounts to almost Rs. 25,000 crore a year. Data on State finances clearly reveal that government wages and salaries (more so university and college teachers salary) are not the main cause of excess government expenditures. Downsizing of government may be desirable for other reasons, but surely the gains in expenditure reduction 'will be small on a proportionate basis. Public investments made in the last 50 years by States have not resulted in providing returns in the form of non-tax revenues to the State governments in India. People in India have got used to not paying adequately for these services on two ground. One is that they perceive that these services are free and second the quality of service being poor, people are not ready to pay higher charges for inefficient service.

It is, therefore, of great importance that imposition of higher user charges has to be accompanied by visible improvements in quality of service provided. Each State government will have to examine each infrastructure sector closely and programme the gradual imposition of economic pricing in each sector. Appointment of independent autonomous regulatory authorities can help in depoliticing the process. This process to be successful needs these authorities to be made autonomous by statute, and the political and bureaucracy authority learn to respect this autonomy.

Retirement of public debt requires generation of large amount of revenue. One major source can be bold privatization of all but strategic public enterprises. Such a bold approach is clearly not easy. The government will first have to clarify the objectives of this approach and seek to forge a consensus across party lines. The objective of such a policy has to be twin based.

(a) Strengthening of these State PSEs to enable them to grow and complete.

(b) Returns from privatization must not be used to meet current revenue expenditures but should explicitly be used for retiring of public debt so that the interest burden of States is progressively reduced.

Public investment by States through the central plan assistance pattern needs reexamination to reduce the problem of growing States' indebtedness to the Centre. Plan loan assistance should depend on economic performance and ability to pay back project wise. Hence loan grant component of plan assistance should have varying proportion projectwise. Projects can be classified into remunerative semi remunerative and non remunerative and the grant loan component made variable on the basis of financial viability of the project.

The above fiscal reform path suggested can be adopted as a five year fiscal correction policy measure. It needs research, public awareness, public education and persuasion. The Central government must take the lead and forge an understanding and consensus with State governments, who must do the same with local bodies. It is because of this that at the outset I mentioned that India today is a fiscally challenged polity. The current fiscal crisis requires a solution that has to be first politically mediated. In these fluid days of coalition governance, States in India to improve their fiscal health need Finance Ministers who are not only visionary but also courageous politician. Unmindful of immediate gains, they will have to draw up fiscal correction plans initiate bold fiscal reforms on both a medium term basis as well as on a long-term perspective plan basis.

The fiscal situation in State finances hence need urgent action and corrective measures on the lines suggested above, in the absence of which the fiscal situation may get worse and will pose a serious threat to economic growth poverty reduction, employment generation and social welfare in the levy near future.

REFERENCES

Bagchi, A., Bajaj, J.L. and Byrd, W.A. (1992), State Finances in India, NIPFP, Vikas Publishing House, New Delhi.

Mundle, S. (ed.), Public Finance: Policy Issues for India, Oxford University Press, New Delhi.

Ministry of Finance, GOI (2000), Report of the Committee on Fiscal Responsibility and Budget Management Bill, 2000, http/fin min.nic.in.

RBI (2000), Report of the Advisory Group on Transparency in Monetary and Fiscal Policies, www.rbi.org.in.

RBI (2000), State Finances: A Study of Budgets of 1999–2000, Reserve Bank of India, Mumbai.

Economic and Political Weekly (2001), Finances of State Governments: Special Statistics, Vol. XXXVI, No. 20, and 21, May 19 June 1.

Rakesh Mohan (2000), Fiscal Correction for Economic Growth: Data Analysis and suggestions,. EPW, Vol. XXXV, No. 24, June.

State Finances (2004), A Study of Budgets of 2003–04, RBI, April.

Tenth Five Year Plan 2002–2007, Planning Commission, Government of India.

16

DISCUSSANT'S REPORT FISCAL AGENDA OF THE STATE GOVTS.

M.C. Kodli

DR. DANGE: FINANCES OF STATE GOVERNMENT IN INDIA

He discussed the status of State Government finances. He emphasised on the growing revenue deficit and fiscal deficit.

To have a 8–9 per cent growth rate, it is essential to increase investment expenditure and capital expenditure of State Governments is crucial in this regard. Increasing borrowings of the State Governments is not resulting into increasing capital expenditure of the state governments.

States outstanding liabilities are increasing at a faster rate. And states are mainly indebted to the Central Government. Market borrowing and loans and advances from the Centre are increasing rapidly. Besides the Central Government gives guarantees to the States' borrowings. The amount of outstanding guarantees as well as its proportion to GDP is increasing.

THERE IS NECESSITY OF LIMIT TO SUCH GUARNATEES

Fiscal Reforms-needs-Multi Directional effort, time frame approach, rule based policy, need for consensus, process of educating the masses of fiscal issues.

- Governments should strictly follow the fiscal measures. He emphasised the following issues:

(i) Fiscal desirability and fiscal practicability.

(ii) Medium term fiscal policy-consistency in fiscal decisions

(iii) Increase in Tax-GDP ratio.

(iv) Increase in non-tax revenue-application and user charges

(v) Composition of public expenditure

REFORM PATH

- Reivew of popular state schemes,
- Reduce non-merit subsidy
- Political consensus
- Emphasis on rural infrastructure
- Public participation in infrastructure development
- He concluded with the remark that the State Governments should strictly follow the fiscal policy.

DR. NARSIMHULU: PAPER PRESENTATION

He briefly discussed the background of new economic policy in India.

We have composite mixed economy in India.

He explained impact of economic reforms on the state governments in India. He overviewed the state finances in India.

Agenda for fiscal reforms in states.

- Expenditure reform-higher salaries-component
- Pension liability increasing
- Reforms in public sector enterprises.
- Tax-GDPO ratio -17.85 Bihar

  8.16 MH

  lowest in Maharashtra
- Fiscal deficit

DISCUSSION

- Dr. Dange has opposed the monopoly purchasing of cotton? But we have to consider the reasons of losses in monopoly procurement of cotton.
- Instead of scrapping the scheme, we should suggest improvement in the scheme.
- Devolution of resources from State to local Government should also be studied in detail.
- State Governments do not give due importance to State Finance corporations.
- Pay Commission's Report and D.A. should not be compulsory to state governments. States should be allowed.
- To have their own pay scales and D.A. etc.

DR. KODLI: CONCLUDING REMARKS

Both the papers are very good and interesting. People in State Governments are not ready to take hard decision either in respect of tax mobilisation or in respect of public expenditure.

RD/GDP-0.3% of GDP in 1985–86 to 4.6% to 1999–2000.

The States have to increase their revenues.

- The nature of plan financing itself led to the increasing states' indebtedness to the Centre.
- Non-tax revenue mobilisation in the state is unsatisfactory-State owned enterprises are incurring increasing losses.
- He concluded with reference to the suggestions given in both the papers.

DR. KULKARNI

Thanks on behalf of the participants.

Dr. Koli extended note of thanks to all the paper presenters and participants.

INDEX

K

L

M